W9-BJR-896

# SHORTCUTS TO EFFECTIVE ON-THE-JOB WRITING

## How to Achieve an Immediate Improvement in Your Business Letters, Memos and Reports

# Lynn Lamphear

Prentice-Hall, Inc., Englewood Cliffs, New Jersey 07632

*Shortcuts to Effective On-the-Job Writing*
by Lynn Lamphear
© 1982 by Lynn Lamphear

Address inquiries to Prentice-Hall, Inc.,
Englewood Cliffs, N.J. 07632
Printed in the United States of America
Prentice-Hall International, Inc., London
Prentice-Hall of Australia, Pty. Ltd., Sydney
Prentice-Hall of Canada, Ltd., Toronto
Prentice-Hall of India Private Ltd., New Delhi
Prentice-Hall of Japan, Inc., Tokyo
Prentice-Hall of Southeast Asia Pt. Ltd., Singapore
Whitehall Books Limited, Wellington, New Zealand
10 9 8 7 6 5 4 3 2 1

ISBN 0-13-809145-5
ISBN 0-13-809137-4 {PBK}

Library of Congress Cataloging in Publication Data
Lamphear, Lynn, date
    Shortcuts to effective on-the-job writing.
    Includes index.
    1. Commercial correspondence.    2. Report writing.
3. Memorandums.    I. Title.
HF5721.L28    808'.066651021    81-21094
                                 AACR2

# TO MY WIFE, DEBBIE

# CONTENTS

Introduction: What Can You Gain From This Book? ..... *ix*

1 Understand Your Writing Attitude .................. *1*

2 Become a Critical Reader.......................... *9*

3 Think About Your Reader ........................ *21*

4 Make Sure You're Understood ..................... *31*

5 Beware of the Jargon Dragon...................... *47*

6 Write Concisely .................................. *60*

7 Adopt an Appropriate Tone....................... *74*

8 Use Effective Paragraphs......................... *87*

9 Develop an Overall Plan......................... *100*

10 Use Effective Openings and Closings ............. *112*

11 Organize Your Material ......................... *128*

12 Punctuate Appropriately ........................ *143*

13 Spell Correctly ................................. *155*

14 Evaluate Your Writing........................... *164*

Index................................................ *173*

# INTRODUCTION

# What Can You Gain From This Book?

Improving your writing skills can help you succeed in whatever job or career you have chosen. The ability to write well is one of the most powerful tools you can use to achieve recognition, job security, and career advancement.

The person who writes well is valued highly in business, industry, government, and education because good writing is so rare. Most on-the-job writing is mediocre in quality; much of it is poor. Given the continuing nationwide decline in writing skills, it's difficult to see much change occurring soon. People possessing these skills increase their value to their organizations.

Effective writing skills can enhance your self-confidence and set you apart from the crowd. Why? Because most people won't spend even a small amount of time to develop, improve, or refine these critical skills. We will spend countless hours watching television or improving our golf game, but we resist or resent the time spent to develop effective letter, memorandum, and report writing skills.

Careers are frequently damaged because many people fail to understand the direct, important relationship between effective written communication skills and career advancement.

What makes written communication so important? Why can't we just "muddle" through?

Consider this: On-the-job writing generates an estimated 40 billion documents a year, probably about 10,000 times more words than the total words of all the fiction published in the United States every year. The bulk of this material consists of letters, memorandums, and reports. These are documents, usually more than one page, that frequently have multiple readers. Multiply 40 billion by the six to ten dollars it takes to generate each piece of paper (depending on whose figures you accept), and we have a staggering statistic. On-the-job writing is big business. In fact, although most organizations don't recognize this, written communication may well be their *primary* business, and selling insurance or manufacturing widgets could be their secondary business.

An estimated 30 percent of on-the-job writing has to be rewritten to correct errors, omissions, or misunderstandings. That's a 30 percent "rejection rate," which doesn't include the written communication problems that are cleared up with telephone calls, meetings, or some other form of communication. Such a high rejection rate, or waste factor, is an enormous drain on organizational productivity that has all too often been accepted as one of the costs of doing business.

It's no wonder, then, that more and more organizations have become aware of the *real* importance of effective written communication—it saves time, it saves money, and it improves the bottom line.

Recognizing the critical importance of effective written communication and taking action to improve your writing skills can give you an advantage in an increasingly competitive work environment. But improving these skills does take time, and time is a precious commodity.

Since you are reading this book, I assume that you want to improve your writing ability and that you want some methods you can apply immediately to the writing you do on your job. Although this book can be used in conjunction with formal writing courses or to supplement more extensive writing textbooks, it's designed primarily for people who need to achieve some tangible writing improvement immediately. It contains "shortcuts" to more effective writing and isn't intended as a replacement for more exhaustive courses or textbooks.

To achieve these shortcuts, I've avoided elaborate explanations and extensive discussions of alternatives. The material concentrates on some *essentials* you need to write more effective letters, memos, and reports. The ideas were distilled from my on-the-job writing experiences as a manager and administrator in business and industry, as a college instructor in business and technical writing, and as a consultant in written communication. I've used these ideas successfully with hundreds of participants in college writing courses and in writing seminars for various organizations.

All of the examples used in this book are *real;* I've selected material from actual letters, memos, and reports to illustrate my points. When you see some of the strange-looking sentences and other writing samples, you may wonder whether I made them up. I didn't. Truth really is stranger than fiction.

You can go through the book from front to back, chapter by chapter, or you can skip around. Each chapter can stand independently, but I think the *overall* method or approach can be grasped much more easily by following the traditional chapter-by-chapter reading.

Many chapters have exercises for you to work. Most exercises are short and give you an opportunity to apply the chapter's writing principles. I encourage you to work these exercises and to check your answers against the examples I've provided.

Some of the techniques will work better than others for you; some you may not feel comfortable with at all. Initially, you may think you won't be able to apply the principles because they would slow you down, and lack of time is always a major factor in on-the-job writing. However, learning to use even a few of these techniques will actually *save* you time because you will be substituting more effective and productive writing habits for less efficient habits.

Remember that 30 percent rejection rate? Time isn't *saved* by producing a document quickly that then fails to do its job efficiently.

Ultimately, of course, for this book of ideas to become valuable to you, you must apply these techniques to *your* on-the-job writing.

Let's get started.

# CHAPTER ONE

# Understand Your Writing Attitude

How do we learn to write letters, memos, and reports—the workhorses of on-the-job writing? Most writing courses in schools—if we took any—concentrate on essay, creative, or book report writing. These writing courses help us develop our writing skills, but they usually don't stress the practical, straightforward, no-frills type of writing we are expected to produce at work.

Unless we are fortunate enough to have taken a formal business writing course, we probably learn how to write letters, memos, and reports *after* we are already on the job. Learning on the job is certainly a valuable way to find out how to do many things; sometimes it's the best or only method for learning how to perform a particular task.

Learning on-the-job writing at work, however, has certain pitfalls. For example, let me relate how I learned to write at work. After graduating from college, I took an administrative position with an insurance company. For several months I managed to avoid writing much of anything, or maybe on-the-job writing avoided me. At any rate, I usually relied on telephone conversations, meetings, or some other form of oral communication to handle my needs.

One day, however, my boss and I took a trip to one of the company's branch offices to gather some information. After we had returned I resumed working in my usual manner, until one afternoon my boss called me on the phone.

"Lamphear, where's that trip report?" he asked.

"What trip report?" I answered.

"Well, we took a trip last week and now you're supposed to write a report to me telling me what we did."

"But you were with me," I protested. "Don't you know what happened?"

"Of course, I know what happened," he shot back, "but we still need a report!"

By the tone of his voice, I knew I was trapped; so I asked him how to write a trip report, since I'd never written one before. (I had submitted by expense voucher for reimbursement of my trip expenses, of course. Getting my money back had seemed like a *sensible* reason for preparing a document.)

My boss didn't hang up the phone, come out of his office, and guide me step by step through my first trip report. Instead, he referred me to the "files" where I would find "the way we do it."

Diligently, I pawed through the files, dug out a few samples, and composed my first on-the-job report. It wasn't very good, but it was "acceptable" (*after* I had explained a few points that weren't clear), and it certainly conformed to "the way we do it."

Although at that time I didn't give it much thought, isn't this experience similar for many of us? Isn't this how many of us learn how to write at work? We imitate what has already been written, either by ransacking the files for some likely examples or by being constantly exposed to enough letters, memos, and reports until we begin to adopt "the way we do it" style without even thinking about it.

Now, there's nothing wrong with imitation. In fact, it's a good way to learn if—and this is a big if—the writer we're imitating is a good writer. Unfortunately, as pointed out in the Introduction to this book, "the way we do it" is usually mediocre, at best.

Our chances of stumbling across some top-notch writers early in our learning process are remote. Much of what we copy will probably have been copied by someone else, who copied it from someone else, and so forth. If this weren't true, we wouldn't see so many phrases and sentences that are worded *exactly* the same way letter after letter, memo after memo, report after report.

This writing pattern can become locked in over time, until we forget that we didn't arrive at our particular writing style through the hard work of trying to sort the good from the bad. We form habits that we question very little. In a sense, we put our writing on automatic pilot.

Since our writing is an extension of ourselves, our egos, we often find it difficult to recognize some of our poorer writing habits, much less attempt to change them. We frequently resent criticism, become defensive, and resist trying something different.

Or perhaps we use another variation of the same theme, such as: "Since that's the way our writing is done here, I can't change it, so why bother? It'll never be acceptable."

Even though most on-the-job writing needs improvement, some of it is *very good*. In every organization I've worked for or with, good writers exist. Their writing is acceptable, and their written communication skills are admired and appreciated. Frequently, what passes as criticism of writing boils down to disagreements over the format to be used, or whether certain information should be revealed, or some other *nonwriting* concern.

I'm sure exceptions exist, but I've seen little hard evidence that good writing is being discriminated against. On the other hand, I have seen the careers of poor writers damaged quite often. Sometimes they never knew why.

Why is understanding your attitude a "shortcut" to more effective writing? Little change will occur unless you take a hard look at some of the things you have been doing and some of the ideas you have about writing on the job. In other words, you have to know "where you're coming from" before you can honestly find out "where you want to go."

Let's begin by examining your writing attitude. Here are some questions for you to answer. Be honest with yourself. Only you know these answers.

Try to answer these questions either "yes" or "no":

1. _____ Do you genuinely like to write?
2. _____ Do you feel that good writing is easy for people who have good writing skills?
3. _____ Do you feel that you have to like writing in order to produce good writing?
4. _____ When you try to write, do you frequently have trouble getting started?
5. _____ Do you think that effective written communication skills are vitally important for your success?
6. _____ After you have written something, are you often asked for additional information?
7. _____ Do people ever say, "I'm not exactly sure what you mean" or "Could you clarify a point for me?" or something similar?
8. _____ Are you often asked to "take another look" or "approach it another way"?
9. _____ Do you usually succeed in *selling* your ideas?
10. _____ Do you usually get the *response* you requested?
11. _____ After receiving an unanticipated response, do you reread your material carefully?
12. _____ Do you feel that it's your reader's responsibility to figure out what your message means?
13. _____ Do you follow up on your letters/memos/reports to find out if your communication was successful?
14. _____ Do you understand your letters/memos/reports when you reread them after a lapse of time?
15. _____ Can you determine why some letters/memos/reports were more effective than others?

1. If you answered "no" to this question, you're definitely in good company. Very few people genuinely like to write at the time they are performing the writing act. Writing is hard work; it forces us to think and then to translate our thoughts onto paper using all kinds of grammatical restrictions. Writing isn't as easy or as natural as speaking.

Many people, however, achieve some measure of satis-faction or sense of accomplishment by struggling with a difficult task and bringing it to a successful conclusion.

You might also consider the kinds of writing you did before writing at work. Many of us learned to write by writing essays or short stories or maybe poems. Early in life we decided we disliked writing because we were "never any good at it." Well, very few people possess the ability or talent to be excellent essayists, novelists, or poets. Good on-the-job writ-ing requires competent writing skills, but it doesn't require you to be above average in talent, creativity, or intelligence. You may never develop a superior style, but you can certainly become a very good writer in the type of writing you do at work.

2. Perhaps good writing is easier for people with good writing skills, but "no," it isn't easy. I'm afraid I can't promise you an easy time of it even if you adhere to all of the principles in this book. The late Agatha Christie, who wrote more than sixty novels, said she always found it difficult to put the right words on a blank piece of paper, no matter how many times she had done it before. Developing good writing skills, however, will permit you to recognize and use certain short-cuts to help you save some time.

3. And "no," you definitely don't have to like to write in order to produce good writing. Nor do you have to be inspired. If we waited for inspiration, very few letters, memos, and reports would ever be written. Writing doesn't have to be "interesting" or "enjoyable" to be competent and worthwhile. A good writer can generate competent writing on any subject. The often mentioned cliché about writing is still true: Good writing results from perspiration, not inspiration.

4. If you answered "yes" to this question, welcome to the group. We all find it difficult to get started at times. Acquiring good habits can help you overcome some problems, but you'll still experience those agonizing periods of "writer's block"

occasionally. If you have never suffered from this common writer's disease, be thankful.

5. I hope you answered "yes" to this question. If you didn't, please reread the Introduction and the first part of this chapter.

6. A "yes" answer means that you're receiving valuable "feedback" (a term we'll discuss in a later chapter). In this case, the feedback indicates that your written communication suffers from omissions or incomplete information.

7. This question also involves feedback. A "yes" answer indicates that your writing lacks "clarity" (more on this term later, too). In other words, you're confusing your readers. Part of the problem could be the result of poorly chosen words or incorrect sentence structures.

8. Another feedback question: "yes" means that you're not getting your point across to your reader. Although these comments are frequently used as "management ploys" when someone wants to avoid making a hard decision or hasn't read your material carefully, you should reexamine your material to make sure you're presenting your points in the most effective way. We'll take a look at some ways to "understand your audience" and "choose an overall plan" in later chapters.

If you answered "no" to questions 6, 7, and 8, your written communication may be effective, or you may be receiving a different set of signals, or you may not be actively "listening" to the feedback, or worst of all from an on-the-job writer's viewpoint, you may not be receiving *any* feedback. You need to always encourage feedback so that you can evaluate your effectiveness.

9. This question involves your effectiveness, but it's also intended to stress the importance of "follow-up" in written communication. A "no" answer means you're not communicating effectively, or you're not following up on your written communication to see what is happening.

10. Again, a "no" answer indicates a lack of effectiveness or lack of follow-up. It's easy to blame "office politics" or "unreceptive or hostile readers" in such cases, but first start with your own written document.

11. If you answered "no" to this question, you're missing another good feedback item. Moreover, a "no" answer shows that you feel the *reader* must be responsible for the foul-up in some way. You might be right, but *you* wrote the document; it probably deserves another look.

12. A "no" answer demonstrates that you recognize it's *your* responsibility to write your message as effectively as you can. Your reader shouldn't be required to interpret or figure out what you're trying to say. If you don't take the care necessary to produce effective written communication, why should your reader treat your document with any greater respect?

A "no" answer to question 11 and a "yes" answer to question 12 indicate that you are "writer"-oriented instead of "reader"-oriented in your approach to written communication. On-the-job writing should always be prepared with the reader in mind, not the writer. After all, we aren't writing those letters, memos, and reports to ourselves. We already know what we're trying to say (I hope). It's the reader we're trying to inform, convince, or persuade.

13. Another follow-up question: "yes" shows you're interested in determining how effective your written communication is; "no" means you're not taking advantage of an excellent evaluation tool.

14. If you answered "no" to this question, try to imagine your reader's plight. If you *never* reread your old material, you're missing another excellent chance to come to grips with some of your writing problems. Using hindsight is a valuable way to spot fouled-up writing because we no longer remember *exactly* what we wrote. If after rereading your material you still aren't sure, think about your poor reader those many weeks or months ago.

15. A "no" answer to this question means you need to develop, improve, or refine your ability to analyze on-the-job writing from a *critical* viewpoint. This book will give you some tools you can use to evaluate your writing in order to produce more effective letters, memos, and reports.

How did you do? Do you feel you have a better handle on your writing attitude? This introductory chapter was designed to start you thinking about written communication and to make you more keenly aware of some problems we all face in trying to write effectively on our jobs.

Let's begin now, in the next chapter, to sharpen your critical eye.

# CHAPTER TWO

# Become a Critical Reader

One of the quickest ways to improve your writing is to become aware of the writing going on around you. Sharpen your "critical" eye by paying closer attention to the writing in the letters, memos, and reports you receive. My own experiences and those of researchers on the writing process have shown that evaluating writing from a critical point of view seems to help people begin to look at their *own* writing more critically.

Becoming a critical reader changes you from a *passive* reader (which most of us are) into an *active* reader and makes you more aware of poor, mediocre, and good writing. Once you begin to think about written communication in terms of "There's a better way to say that," or "That's not a very effective sentence," or "I wonder why this word was used," you're on your way to making substantial improvements in your own writing.

Let's do some exercises to help you look at writing more critically. The groups of sentences below have been evaluated by over five hundred people who write letters, memos, and reports on their jobs. They were asked to determine which sentence in each set is the *most effective* and which is the *least effective.* To perform this analysis correctly, they had to consider what the original writers of these sentences were trying to accomplish by writing four versions of the same message in each set.

After you've worked the exercises, I'll tell you which sentences were chosen as the most effective by the majority of people who evaluated them. I'll also give you some of the reasons for the choices.

In each set of sentences circle the *most* effective statement and the *least* effective statement. Consider what the writer is trying to accomplish.

1. a. We are in receipt of yours of the 15th.
   b. Have received your letter of April 15.
   c. We've received your letter of April 15.
   d. We wish to acknowledge receipt of your letter of April 15.
   e. We've received your April 15 letter.

2. a. We have your check for $15 and wish to thank you for it.
   b. Thank you for your check for $15.
   c. Your check for $15 received and acknowledged with thanks.
   d. Thank you for your $15 check.
   e. Have received check in the amount of $15 and thank you for same.

3. a. Enclosed is our annual report.
   b. Our annual report is enclosed.
   c. Enclosed herewith is our annual report.
   d. Please find enclosed our annual report.
   e. I'm enclosing our annual report.

4. a. These are our terms and all our customers must live up to them.
   b. These terms must be enforced because we would lose money if we made exceptions.
   c. Our terms are the same for all customers.
   d. Surely, you would not expect us to grant special privileges to you.

5. a. The shirt was unmistakably worn.
   b. The shirt shows signs of wear.
   c. Evidently, you wore the shirt before you decided to return it.
   d. There's no doubt that you wore the shirt.

6. a. We're sorry our blunder caused you such inconvenience.
   b. We're sorry our error caused you such inconvenience.
   c. We're sorry our "goof" caused you such inconvenience.
   d. We're sorry our silly mistake caused you such inconvenience.

7. a. You will hear from us as soon as we have checked you out.
   b. You will hear from us as soon as we have investigated your background.
   c. You will hear from us as soon as we have reviewed your information.
   d. You will hear from us as soon as we have verified what you told us.

8. a. Your analysis of the problem is wrong.
   b. Your analysis of the problem is incorrect.
   c. Your analysis of the problem is off base.
   d. Your analysis of the problem is not right.

9. a. We're sorry for the misunderstanding.
   b. We're sorry you misunderstood us.
   c. We're sorry you seem to have misunderstood us.
   d. We're sorry for the mutual misunderstanding.

10. a. Your payment is delinquent.
    b. Your payment is not up-to-date.
    c. Your payment is overdue.
    d. Your payment is in arrears.

11. a. We are forced to refuse your request.
    b. We are unable to grant your request.
    c. We must turn down your request.
    d. Your request is denied.

12. a. It's against our policy to cash checks for over $100.
    b. It's our policy to cash checks for $100 and under.
    c. Our policy is to cash checks for $100 and under.
    d. Our policy is to not cash checks for over $100.

13. a. We're sorry to tell you that the alterations won't be completed until Friday.
    b. Unfortunately, the alterations won't be completed until Friday.
    c. Hopefully, the alterations will be completed by Friday.
    d. The alterations will be completed by Friday.

14. a. We should utilize these facilities to the ultimate degree.
    b. We should use these facilities as much as possible.
    c. We should maximize utilization of these facilities.
    d. These facilities should be maximally utilized by us.

15. a. Increasing the visual access to the runway, we should illuminate it greater.
    b. In order to increase our visibility of the runway, we should raise the lighting level.
    c. For us to visualize the runway better, we should elevate the intensity of the lights.
    d. To see the runway better, we should turn up the lights.

16. a. The purpose of this report is to present information about the dangers of unsafe drinking water.
    b. This report contains information about the dangers of unsafe drinking water.
    c. The dangers of unsafe drinking water are contained in this report.
    d. The information presented in this report is about the dangers of unsafe drinking water.

17. a. Deliver one ton of salt each Tuesday for five consecutive weeks, beginning October 6.
    b. For five consecutive weeks beginning October 6, deliver one ton of salt.
    c. Beginning October 6, deliver five tons of salt each Tuesday in one-ton lots for five consecutive weeks.
    d. One ton of salt should be delivered each Tuesday for five consecutive weeks beginning October 6.

18. a. This company was founded in 1947 as an aircraft manufacturer and then diversified into computers in 1965.
    b. This aircraft manufacturing company, founded in 1947, diversified into computers in 1965.
    c. Founded in 1947, this aircraft manufacturing company diversified into computers in 1965.
    d. This aircraft manufacturing company diversified into computers in 1965 and was founded in 1947.

19. a. The outer wall is red in color, 15 feet wide, made of concrete, and is 10 feet high.
    b. The outer wall is 15 feet wide, 10 feet high, red, and concrete.
    c. The outer, red, concrete wall is 15 feet wide and 10 feet high.
    d. The concrete wall is red, 15 feet wide, and 10 feet high.

20. a. Since John lost his tools last month, he hasn't been able to work as a mechanic.
    b. While John lost his tools last month, he hasn't been able to work as a mechanic.
    c. Because John lost his tools last month, he hasn't been able to work as a mechanic.
    d. Even though John lost his tools last month, he hasn't been able to work as a mechanic.

After deciding on the *most effective* statement, the majority of people found it more difficult to select the *least effective* statement from the remaining sentences. In addition, some people came up with even more effective ways to put these messages across. In a few cases the most effective statement isn't necessarily the "best" way to handle the situation; it's simply better than the other choices.

1. *Most effective:* c or e    *Least effective:* b
A simple acknowledgment can be expressed concisely as in either "c" or "e." Sentence "b" isn't a complete sentence (no

subject). Both "a" and "d" use old-fashioned, trite wording that has been copied over and over again from someone's old, musty file. Sentence "a" doesn't identify what "yours" is, and "d" uses a "wind-up" phrase ("wish to acknowledge") instead of just simply getting to the point. In general, try to avoid overusing "I would like to," "I want to," and "I wish to."

**2.** *Most effective:* d  *Least effective:* e
Another acknowledgment message that can be expressed directly and concisely as in "d." Sentence "b" is also good, but why use the preposition "for" twice? Sentences "a," "c," and "e" all fall into the same wordy pattern: they acknowledge receipt of the check and *then* thank the sender. Two actions aren't required; the "thank you" takes care of both. Sentence "e" is the least effective because it isn't a complete sentence (no subject).

**3.** *Most effective:* b or e  *Least effective:* c
Enclosure messages should be expressed in a *natural* way, such as "b" or "e." Sentence "e" can be very effective if you're trying to achieve a more personal tone. Sentence "a" is not as effective because the normal word order is reversed ("enclosed is ... " instead of " ... is enclosed"). Still, "a" is far better than "c" and "d," which are examples of "musty file" writing. Neither *sounds* natural, the way someone might express these messages in speech. They sound artificial and stuffy. When was the last time you used "herewith" in a conversation with anyone? That word probably helped sentence "c" edge out "d" in the least effective category, although "d" shows up more often.

**4.** *Most effective:* c  *Least effective:* b
Sentence "c" is the most *tactful* way of expressing this message. All of the other sentences show a lack of consideration for the reader. Sentence "a" takes the autocratic approach—you *must* live up to *our terms*—although I'm not sure how someone "lives up" to a term or condition. Sentence "b" is the worst because the writer is "enforcing" (very negative word) terms for a reason the reader doesn't care anything about, and the writer probably shouldn't reveal to

the reader anyway. The word "surely" in sentence "d" makes the statement sound sarcastic.

5. *Most Effective:* b    *Least effective:* c
Another message requiring some degree of tact. Sentence "b" gets the point across without necessarily stomping on someone's toes. Sentences "a" and "d" are direct, but they are also curt and sound like accusations. Sentence "c" also sounds like an accusation, but it adds a sarcastic element with the word "evidently." Some people "hear" sarcasm in *ly* words that begin sentences, particularly if the rest of the message refers to them ("Obviously, you didn't … " or "Surely, you wouldn't expect…").

6. *Most effective:* b    *Least effective:* c *or* d
"Error" is a softer word than "blunder," and it gets the message across; thus, "b" is more effective than "a." Sentences "c" and "d" have the same problem: they're inappropriate for on-the-job writing. "Goof" is a slang expression, and even though the writer sets the word off with quotation marks, it's still not good writing. The word "silly" should be avoided as well because it sounds childish. Sentences "c" and "d" could also trigger a negative reaction from the reader because they make light of the reader's inconvenience.

7. *Most effective:* c    *Least effective:* a
Sentence "c" is much less threatening to the reader, but it puts across the point that some sort of checking will be done. Sentence "a" sounds as if the reader will be run around a racetrack or something. At any rate, it's not appropriate on-the-job writing. Sentence "b" uses another one of those negative words—"investigated." Most people don't like to be "investigated" or "interrogated" or to be considered "delinquent" (as in juvenile delinquent). We also aren't overjoyed to have our statements "verified" (sentence "d") because that smacks of lack of trust on someone's part.

8. *Most effective:* b    *Least effective:* c
Another word choice exercise. "Incorrect" (sentence "b") is a more tactful way to tell someone that he or she is "wrong" (sentence "a") or "not right" (sentence "d"). "Off base" (sen-

tence "c"), on the other hand, is slang, and it sounds as if the reader missed the point completely; or to use another slang expression, the reader was "way out in left field."

9. *Most effective:* a    *Least effective:* b
This exercise involves "eggshell" writing, which is the most difficult kind of tactful writing. If you're trying to be *super-tactful,* choose sentence "a." It's the only statement in this batch that avoids casting blame. We can probably agree that we've had a "misunderstanding" as long as the fault remains anonymous. However, sentences "b" and "c" put the blame on the reader (the word "seem" in "c" makes this statement a little better than "b"). Sentence "d" ("mutual misunderstanding") is generous of the writer, but it still puts at least part of the blame on the reader.

By the way, the word "sorry" can be used very effectively in on-the-job writing because it has a double meaning. It can mean that you're "apologizing" for something ("I'm sorry I made this mistake in my report") or that you're identifying or sympathizing with the reader without necessarily assuming guilt ("I'm sorry you broke your leg last week"). Exercise 9 uses "I'm sorry" effectively, especially in sentence "a," because the writer takes advantage of the double meaning to smooth over a ticklish situation. "Eggshell" writing without "giving away the store."

10. *Most effective:* c    *Least effective:* a
Sentence "c" expresses the message accurately and tactfully. Sentence "a" uses one of those negative words—"delinquent." Sentences "b" and "d" aren't worded as accurately as "c," even though they're more tactful than "a."

11. *Most effective:* b    *Least effective:* a
None of these sentences is perfect, but "b" comes closest to combining tact with the negative message. I've always been uncomfortable with the word "unable" when it's used to deny something that, in fact, I was "able" to do but didn't want to for some reason. However, I'm not sure most people view the word that literally. Sentence "a" is the worst of the lot because

of the word "forced," which implies that someone made us do something against our will. We aren't "forced" to deny requests; we deny them because of company policy or some other reason. Sentence "c" sounds softer than "d." Sentence "d" ("Your request is denied") is probably the most direct way of refusing a request, but it sounds arbitrary and autocratic. I can almost see a huge rubber stamp with the words REQUEST DENIED poised in the air, ready to strike.

12. *Most effective:* c   *Least effective:* a
Whenever possible, it's always better to express messages in a positive way. Why be negative if we don't have to be? Sentence "c" uses this positive approach. Sentence "b" is also positive, but what's gained by putting the word "it's" at the beginning of the sentence? Sentences "a" and "d" take the negative approach, but "a" has another one of those negative words— "against." This word sets up a barrier between writer and reader. We have to use it sometimes to get our message across; but it's a word that should be used sparingly.

13. *Most effective:* d   *Least effective:* c
Another example of unnecessary negative writing. Since we've already missed the deadline, why not try to salvage as much goodwill as possible? Sentence "d" takes an upbeat, positive approach. Sentence "a" is less negative than "b" because "a" avoids combining the negative expression ("won't") with another negative word ("unfortunately"). Sentence "c" introduces an element of doubt about whether the situation is under control; the writer doesn't seem to be sure.

14. *Most effective:* b   *Least effective:* d
This set of sentences deals with "jargon" and how we can get carried away with "utilizing," "maximizing," and "ultimate-degreeing" things. Sentence "b" expresses the message in the most straightforward, natural way. I doubt that any of us would actually use any of the other statements if we were *speaking* to someone. They sound "puffed up" because the language has been unnecessarily elevated. Sentence "d" shows how tortured this type of writing can become.

15. *Most effective:* d    *Least effective:* a
Another example of elevating the language beyond what's necessary to get the message across effectively. Sentence "d" avoids "visualizing" and "illuminating" and "elevating intensities" by using down-to-earth words such as "see" and "turn up." If you think that using short, direct words in place of elevated words doesn't sound as "educated," take a look at sentence "a." The words may be "bigger," but the writer ends up with a poor sentence that makes little sense. In addition, notice how wordy sentences "b" and "c" are.

16. *Most effective:* b    *Least effective:* c
Sentence "b" is the most straightforward statement. Sentences "a" and "d" use *unnecessary* words before getting to the point ("The purpose of this report is to..." and "The information presented in this report is about..."). Yes, sentence "c" is the most concise, but it doesn't make any sense. The sentence literally says that the "dangers of unsafe drinking water" are physically "contained" in the report. I hope they're well contained because I wouldn't want them to escape.

17. *Most effective:* a    *Least effective:* c
Sentence "a" puts the ideas in their correct order. First tell *what* you want and then tell *when* you want it. Sentence "d" is also good, but "a" is expressed in *active voice* (more about this later), which is always more direct ("Deliver" vs. "should be delivered"). Sentence "b" leaves out "Tuesday," but sentence "c" is written poorly and could confuse the reader ("deliver five tons of salt each Tuesday" isn't accurate).

18. *Most effective:* b *or* c    *Least effective:* d
We could probably debate the merits of where to place "founded in 1947" in the sentence; however, I can see a case for either version. Both "b" and "c" put the ideas in their correct order: the founding came first; then came the diversification. Sentence "a" also uses the correct order, but it's not as well written. Sentence "d" gets the major ideas backward.

19. *Most effective:* b    *Least effective:* a

Even though sentence "b" is usually chosen as the most effective in this set, I'm not convinced that "c" and "d" aren't as effective. The reason for selecting "b" is solid, though: first mention the item you're going to describe ("outer wall") and *then* describe it. Notice how "c" and "d" split the description ("c" makes the color and material *part of* of the item and then gives the measurements; "d" makes the material *part of* the item and then gives the color and measurements). In a short description this "mixing" doesn't confuse the reader, but it might in a more detailed description. Sentence "a," on the other hand, shows how poorly organized even a few details can be. Look at the unnecessary words, too ("red *in color*" and "*made of* concrete").

20. *Most effective:* c    *Least effective:* b *or* d

Sentence "c" is the only sentence that won't confuse the reader. Sentence "a" has a double meaning (does "since" mean "because" or "from the time"?). We may *assume* we know which meaning the writer intended, but we can't be sure. Sentences "b" and "d" don't make much sense because "while" and "even though" are used incorrectly.

These exercises have touched on many of the writing guidelines I'll be discussing in later chapters: conciseness, clarity, jargon, tone, audience analysis, idea organization, and writing mechanics.

You can apply your "critical eye" to any kind of writing to help you improve your own writing by making you more *selective* in the language you use to express your messages.

*Exercises*

Here are some additional exercises for you to work on. I'll give you the answers at the end of the chapter.

Write sentences for the following messages:

1. Enclose a check for $25 in a letter.
2. Acknowledge receiving a report about hazardous waste control.

3. Acknowledge receiving a customer's complaint letter, dated June 15.

4. Apologize for a mistake you've made in figuring up someone's hospital bill.

5. Someone has been inconvenienced. Don't apologize, but sympathize with the person.

6. Tell someone that you can't complete your report until August 30.

7. Tell someone that your store isn't open after 5 P.M.

8. Ask someone to deliver 30 television sets, 5 at a time, every Monday for 6 consecutive weeks, beginning November 12.

9. Ask someone to deactivate the air conditioning before he or she leaves the premises.

10. Tell someone that it's against your company's policy for your employees to work more than a 40-hour week.

*Answers to Exercises*

1. A $25 check is enclosed. (I'm enclosing a $25 check.)

2. I've received the hazardous waste control report.

3. I've received your June 15 letter. (I've received your letter of June 15.)

4. I apologize for my mistake in figuring your hospital bill. (I apologize for your incorrect hospital bill.)

5. I'm sorry you were inconvenienced.

6. I'll complete my report by August 30.

7. We're open until 5 P.M.

8. Please deliver 5 television sets each Monday for 6 consecutive weeks, beginning November 12.

9. Please turn off the air conditioner before you leave.

10. Our policy is that our employees work only 40 hours a week.

# CHAPTER THREE

# Think About Your Reader

This chapter emphasizes the basic concept behind successful on-the-job writing: We write for our readers, not for ourselves.

As I mentioned in Chapter One, we already know what we're *trying* to say. Our task is to get our thoughts onto paper. If we don't do that correctly, we're not communicating with our reader. And if we're not communicating, why bother to write in the first place?

In a sense, as on-the-job writers we're more fortunate than other writers because we usually know *something* about our readers (our "audience"). Sometimes we know a great deal. Can we take advantage of this knowledge to become better writers? Definitely.

Many people rarely think about their readers; they write to themselves. Consequently, they're frequently surprised when their letters, memos, and reports aren't received or understood the way they thought they would be. It's tempting to blame the reader for our failure to communicate our message properly, but the writer bears this responsibility because the writer initiated the message.

Take a look at the diagram on the next page. This diagram could fit any type of communication process that involves sending messages, but we're going to use it to discuss written communication. There are many versions of this diagram (some of them can be quite complex), but the underlying process is the same: The *writer* initiates a *message* that is sent through a *channel* (in our case, a written document) to a *reader* with the aim of achieving some *effect* (to inform, persuade, convince, etc.).

This process sounds easy enough: All we have to do is write to our reader, and then our reader will be informed, persuaded, convinced, or whatever. But this communication process is constantly attacked by *interference* (sometimes called *static* or *noise*) that can distort the message and confuse the reader. As writers, our responsibility is to help our readers understand our messages by eliminating as much interference as we can.

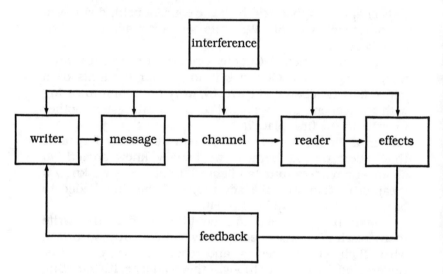

Some of this interference can be caused by excessive wordiness, confusing jargon, unclear words or sentences, poorly organized ideas, inappropriate tone, poor spelling, or incorrect punctuation. I'll discuss these interference problems and ways to avoid them in later chapters.

But failure to *think about* our reader also ranks as a major interference problem.

For example, let's look at an exchange of letters between a bank employee and a savings account depositor who wants some information about making a withdrawal by mail.

The depositor wrote the following letter:

I'm on vacation in Florida, and I need some information about how to withdraw money from my savings account.

I'd like to withdraw $200 every month for the next three months. I brought my passbook with me. Please tell me what to do.

The bank employee wrote the following answer:

We cannot honor your withdrawal request at this time. While we do permit withdrawals by mail, our bank has very strict regulations about such withdrawals. They can be made only with a signed withdrawal slip and presentation of the passbook.

At first glance, the bank employee's letter might appear to take care of the situation. But it didn't. The letter irritated the depositor and prompted the depositor to write another letter to the bank.

I received your letter of November 10 today. First of all, I wasn't making a withdrawal request in my letter of November 2. I was asking for some *information* about mail withdrawals.

Secondly, I'm in Florida, not Missouri. I told you in my first letter that I had my passbook, but I don't have a supply of withdrawal slips. Since it's such a *strict regulation* that I have to fill out the slip, why don't you send me some?

The bank employee received valuable *feedback* (see the diagram) in this second letter. This feedback indicates that the bank employee wasn't thinking about the depositor when answering the first letter. The letter was written from the *writer's* point of view, not the reader's.

The writer was more interested in telling the depositor about the bank's policy instead of *explaining* how that policy actually protects the depositor's savings account from unauthorized withdrawals, and then *helping* the depositor comply with the policy by sending a supply of withdrawal slips.

A more appropriate reply to the depositor's first letter might go something like this:

> Yes, you can certainly make withdrawals from your savings account by mail.
>
> For your protection, please send your passbook and a signed withdrawal slip with each withdrawal request. Your signature authorizes us to make the necessary withdrawals from your account.
>
> I'm enclosing some withdrawal slips and postpaid envelopes. We should be able to process your request the same day we receive it.

Notice the *reader-oriented* writing in this letter. The writer still makes the point that the bank must have the necessary documents before the reader's request can be processed. But the bank's "strict regulations" are now for the reader's protection as well as the bank's. In addition, the writer supplies the reader with the required forms, thus *anticipating* what the reader will need.

The writer thinks about the reader by asking and answering a few important questions:

Who is my reader? *a savings account depositor*

What does my reader want? *to withdraw funds by mail*

What does my reader need? *information, a passbook, withdrawal slips, and postpaid envelopes*

What does my reader have already? *a passbook*

How can I help my reader? *send information, withdrawal slips, and postpaid envelopes*

Was it important for the bank employee to think about the depositor before answering the depositor's first letter? Well, consider the results from the original "nonthinking" letter. The bank's customer became irritated, as I think we can tell from the tone of the second letter. Irritating customers (or anyone, for that matter) isn't good business practice, particularly if the handling of a *routine situation* causes the irritation. Beyond the "ruffled feathers" consider the duplication of effort required to straighten out the situation. Four letters were written, instead of just two, and the whole business took at least an extra week to ten days to resolve (not very productive or profitable for the bottom line).

Even though you and your reader haven't had any previous contact (as was the case in our example), you can still think about your reader (*analyze your audience*) and come up with valuable information that will make your letters, memos, and reports more effective.

Frequently, however, we're much more familiar with our readers, especially when writing to people inside our organizations. In these instances, you can ask yourself more questions about your readers and probably come up with more detailed answers. You won't always be able to analyze your audience thoroughly, but even a few answers will help make your writing more effective.

Here are some basic questions that might serve as a checklist to help you start thinking about your reader. I'm sure you can add many other questions or adapt these questions to suit your audience.

1. Who is my reader?
   Position/title/rank
   Relationship to my organization/department/
   section/etc.
   Relationship to me
   Attitude toward my organization/department/
   section/etc.
   Attitude toward me
   Personal characteristics
   Technical expertise
2. Have we corresponded about this subject before?
   Reader's knowledge about the subject
   Reader's attitude toward the subject
   Points we agree on
   Points we disagree on
   Any other significant items
3. What does my reader want?
   Information/ideas/analysis/etc.

Opinion/suggestion/recommendation/decision/action/etc.

Materials/supplies/funds/etc.

4. Why does my reader want it?
5. When does my reader want it?
6. What does my reader need?
7. Why does my reader need it?
8. When does my reader need it?
9. How much does my reader know already?
10. What does my reader have already?
11. How can I help my reader?
12. What effect upon my reader should my letter/memo/proposal/report have?

Do I expect a reply? What kind? When?

Do I expect an opinion/suggestion/recommendation/decision/etc.?

Do I expect my reader to do something? What? How? When?

Do I expect a negative, neutral, or positive reaction to my letter/memo/proposal/report? Why?

Once you've completed your "thinking" process, your *language* can show that you're considering your reader's point of view. For example, notice the difference in the use of pronouns between the first and second versions of our bank employee's letter:

*We* cannot honor your withdrawal request at this time. While *we* do permit withdrawals by mail, *our* bank has very strict regulations about such withdrawals. They can be made only with a signed withdrawal slip and presentation of the passbook.

Yes, *you* can certainly make withdrawals from *your* savings account by mail.

For *your* protection, please send *your* passbook and a signed withdrawal slip with each withdrawal request. *Your* signature authorizes us to make the necessary withdrawals from *your* account.

I'm enclosing some withdrawal slips and postpaid

envelopes. We should be able to process *your* request the same day we receive it.

I've italicized the key pronouns that make the first letter *writer-oriented* and the second letter *reader-oriented*. Stressing the "we" in the first letter gives the impression that the bank's rules are more important than the depositor's needs ("We cannot honor..." "We do permit...").

Emphasizing "you" in the second letter shows that the bank is concerned about providing service to the depositor. Most of us are more interested in how something will benefit us. However, shifting to the "you" attitude doesn't mean the bank "gave away the store." The same rules are in the second letter.

Here are some examples to show you the differences between writer-oriented and reader-oriented writing.

### The You Approach vs. the We Approach

Notice the position of the "we" in the first sentence of each pair: "we" always appears *before* "you" or "your" appears. Shifting the "you" or "your" to the beginning of the sentence makes the message more reader-oriented.

1. *We* have enclosed an envelope for your convenience.

For *your* convenience, we've enclosed an envelope.

2. *We* will be glad to ship *our* order to you as soon as we know what sizes you want.

*Your* order will be shipped as soon as *you* tell us what sizes *you* want.

3. *We* permit a 5 percent discount for payments in cash.

*You're* entitled to a 5 percent discount if *you* pay in cash.

### The You Approach vs. the Impersonal Approach

Most of us like to feel that we're being addressed "personally" instead of just being a face in the crowd. The "you" approach can turn those "everybody" messages into more personal messages.

1. *A* good credit rating can be *a person's* most valuable asset.

*Your* good credit rating can be *your* most valuable asset.

2. *Employee's* suggestions are always appreciated.

*Your* suggestions are always appreciated.

3. *Our customers* are invited to stop in and see our fine line of washing machines.

*You're* invited to stop in and see our fine line of washing machines.

### The Reader's Point of View vs. the Writer's Point of View

In most on-the-job situations the writer *and* the reader have something to gain or lose. Emphasizing how the reader will benefit (instead of stressing your needs) can make your writing more effective because it shows that you've considered the situation from your reader's point of view. Most of us feel less threatened and respond more favorably if we feel the other person understands our interests, needs, etc.

1. *To help us* update *our* monthly inventory and to keep you informed about the status of your order, please complete the enclosed form.

*To keep you informed* about the status of *your* order, please complete the enclosed form.

2. *I need* your report so that *I can* get *my report* finished.

*Your report* is *a key piece of information* for my report.

3. *Our* new *vacuum cleaner* is *the best model we've*

ever *made* because it can cut household vacuuming time in half and costs less to operate.

*You can save* time and money with our new vacuum cleaner.

*Thinking about* your reader is always important in any on-the-job writing situation so that you can anticipate interference problems that might damage the effectiveness of your message. Learning to use reader-oriented language can help you show that you've considered the situation from your reader's point of view. But a word of caution: *Every sentence* shouldn't stress the "you" approach, particularly when this approach might make you appear insincere. Overusing any writing technique isn't a good idea; you should always strive for some degree of balance.

However, despite my caution, exposure to on-the-job writing has convinced me that most of us have some distance to go before we *overuse* the "you" approach. We're too used to writing from our own point of view.

*Exercises*
Rewrite the following sentences so that they emphasize the "you" approach.

1. We would like to take this opportunity to thank you for accepting our job offer.

2. We were happy to receive your order for ten Model 807 saw blades.

3. We shipped your walnut desk this morning; it should arrive in ten days.

4. I have approved your request to take your vacation during July.

5. Our new refrigerators are guaranteed for ten years, so our customers can be sure they're getting a quality appliance.

6. The enclosed pamphlet explains the new federal and state estate taxes.

7. We need your check for $409.50 to cover your overdue charge account bill.

8. A person can qualify for our accounting position by having two years of cost accounting experience.

9. I'm gratified to see an employee who takes an interest in the work.

10. We'd appreciate your roofing business right now because business is somewhat slow.

## Answers to Exercises

1. Thank you for accepting our job offer.

2. Thank you for your order for ten Model 807 saw blades. (Your order for ten Model 807 saw blades is appreciated.)

3. Your walnut desk should arrive in ten days.

4. Your vacation request is approved.

5. Your new refrigerator will have a ten-year guarantee, so you can be sure you're getting a quality appliance.

6. Your estate planning can be simplified if you read the enclosed pamphlet. (You can get help with your estate taxes by reading the enclosed pamphlet.)

7. Sending your check for $409.50 will help you maintain your good credit.

8. You can qualify for our accounting position if you have two years of cost accounting experience.

9. Your interest in your work is gratifying.

10. Your roofing needs will receive our closest attention.

# CHAPTER FOUR

# Make Sure You're Understood

Making sure that your reader understands your message requires you to pay close attention to the *clarity* of your writing. Clear writing can be understood easily because it isn't confusing or misleading. Clarity involves using specific words for general words, using correct words for "almost" correct words, and maintaining sentence unity.

Unclear writing is a major interference problem that frequently causes misunderstandings. Sometimes we *think* we understand what the writer is trying to say, but upon a closer look we're not quite sure.

Look at this sentence, for example:

"Under difficult circumstances our company has been obligated to change its policy due to increasing economic situations."

I think we can determine that the company has had some sort of problem that required it to change its policy. But that's about all we can figure out, although the sentence *appears* to tell us much more. For instance, we don't know what *caused* the change in policy, even though the writer tells us the change was "due to increasing economic situations."

What is an "increasing economic situation"? I've heard of *good* situations and *bad* situations, but I don't know what an *increasing* situation is. Situations can be *better, worse, difficult,* or *confusing,* but they don't *increase* or *decrease.* The misuse of the word "increasing" confuses this message and forces us to guess what the writer means (inflation? cost overruns? more debt?, etc.).

Of course, the words "economic situations" don't tell us anything because they're not precise enough. Exactly what are these "economic situations"? The words are too general, too vague; they lack concrete *meaning*.

The words "under difficult circumstances" are also vague and don't actually tell us what those circumstances were or why they were difficult. However, these words aren't as significant to the *content* of the message, which seems to be that *something* ("increasing economic situations") *caused* the company to change its policy.

Unless we ask the person who wrote this sentence to clarify it for us, we can never be sure that we fully understand it. If the writer didn't want the reader to understand this sentence, then the writer succeeded. But "blue smoke" writing (*deliberately* confusing the reader) is easy to do and has nothing to do with *communicating* messages.

Many things can cause unclear writing, but poor word choices, incorrect or confusing sentences, wordiness, and jargon are major stumbling blocks. In this chapter I'll discuss word choices and sentences from the viewpoint of making them more precise. Wordiness and jargon also involve word choices and sentence structures, but they deserve chapters of their own.

Let's start with word choices. Here are some suggestions to help you make sure you're understood.

### Use the Correct Word

Many words are confused and misused because they're similar in either spelling or meaning. But "similar" and "correct" aren't interchangeable at the whim of the writer. It's one thing to come up with another word that has a similar meaning (icy/frozen), but it's incorrect to use word pairs such as affect/effect, infer/imply, or disorganized/unorganized as if each word in the pair means the same as the other word.

Here are ten frequently confused and misused word pairs. Read each sentence and pick the correct word. I'll give you the answers at the end of the exercise.

1. The constant noise in the office affected/effected his ability to concentrate.
2. Our company used fewer/less barrels of oil this year.
3. She inferred/implied from the economist's speech that prices weren't going to decrease.
4. My instructions on this assignment were explicit/implicit.
5. The interest on your principal/principle is $40.78.
6. When I returned after my vacation, I found my office completely disorganized/unorganized.
7. If I have to go to court, I hope the judge is disinterested/uninterested.
8. How much farther/further you can develop depends on your motivation.
9. Do you know if/whether the committee has agreed?
10. Mrs. Williams is eminently/imminently qualified to become a judge.

1. "Affected" is the correct word. These two words are often confused and misused. "Affect" is a *verb* meaning to influence. "Effect" is a *noun* meaning the result of something (The *effects* of the storm were severe). Affect/effect have other meanings, but most of the confusion occurs when "effect" is used incorrectly as a verb meaning to influence.

2. "Fewer" is correct. "Fewer" is used with items that can be counted. "Less" is used with items that can't be counted (I have less *motivation* or less *time* or less *need*, etc.).

3. "Inferred" is the right word. "Infer" means to draw a conclusion from what someone else said. "Imply" means to suggest something (She *implied* that she wouldn't show up on time).

4. "Explicit" is correct. "Explicit" means that something is expressed in a definite way, such as a set of instructions. "Implicit" is used with assumptions, impressions, or some-

thing that isn't directly stated (It was *implicit* from the tone of his voice that he wasn't pleased with me).

5. "Principal" is the right word. "Principal" means *money* in this example. It can also mean *main* or *chief* (The principal reason, principal idea, principal factor, etc.). Then, there is the *principal* of a high school. "Principle" refers to a rule or standard of conduct (He had very high *principles*). It's also used to express fundamental guidelines, such as the *principles* of biology.

6. "Disorganized" is the correct word. "Disorganized" is used with things that were organized but now have been disturbed. "Unorganized" is used with things that have never been organized before (The company's mailing list was *unorganized* because it was just a random accumulation of names and addresses).

7. "Disinterested" is the right word. "Disinterested" means impartial, unbiased, or neutral. "Uninterested" means lack of interest (James was so *uninterested* in the lecture that he fell asleep).

8. "Further" is correct. "Further" means additional. "Farther" refers to physical, *measurable* distance (The city is six miles *farther*).

9. "Whether" is right. "Whether" indicates some sort of alternative (the committee either has agreed or has not agreed). "If" indicates a condition in which there is *no alternative* (What will we do *if* the committee agrees?).

10. "Eminently" is the correct word. "Eminent" means conspicuous, noteworthy, outstanding, distinguished, or renowned. "Imminent" means that something is about to happen or likely to happen (The storm is imminent).

Perhaps you found some of your favorites in this exercise. There are many more words that are confused and misused frequently; I'll give you another batch at the end of this chapter.

### Use Specific Words Instead of General Words
Sometimes we know more about a subject than we reveal in our messages. We often use vague or general words that carry

very little meaning. Vague words either leave the reader in the dark or require *additional* words to put across the message. When you know the details, try to use *specific* wording that has some "meat" in it.

1. *Considerable money* could be saved if we manufactured *part of this product* ourselves. (general)

We could save *over $5,000* a year if we manufactured the *window frames* ourselves. (specific)

2. Delivery of *your order* will be delayed *for a time* because of *some difficulties* we're having. (general)

Delivery of *your May 15 order* will be delayed until *August 15* because of *a shortage of valve stems.* (specific)

3. Purchase orders *in large amounts* should be countersigned by *a department head.* (general)

Purchase orders for *over $10,000* should be countersigned by the *purchasing manager, accounts payable manager, or facilities manager.* (specific)

### Use Precise Words Instead of "Almost" Precise Words
Actually, I'm not sure what an "almost" precise word is; either a word is the right one for the job or it's not. However, I think these examples will illustrate how we can come *close* to using the exact or precise words but still miss.

1. Our office has pleasant *atmospheric conditions* that encourage creative work. ("Atmospheric conditions" are clouds, rain, snow, etc.)

Our office has a pleasant *atmosphere* that encourages creative work.

2. We've received your *amount* for $33.45 in payment of our invoice. ($33.45 *is* the "amount").

We've received your *check* for $33.45 in payment of our invoice.

3. The *price* of this stock is *selling* high. (How can a "price" *sell* high, low, or anything?)

This *stock* is *selling* at a *high price.*

### Avoid Ambiguous Wording

Ambiguous wording can confuse a reader because the message takes on a *double meaning* or an *unintended meaning.* Sometimes ambiguous wording leaves us up in the air—we don't know exactly what the writer is trying to say. Usually, the writer can't see the double or unintended meaning until it's pointed out.

1. This new Davidson chair will *eliminate tired employees.* (I don't think I'd like to sit in this chair. "Eliminate" sounds rather permanent.)

This new Davidson chair will *reduce employee fatigue.*

2. I don't know Mr. Phillips *as well as Mr. Lewis.* (Do I know Lewis better than I know Phillips *or* does Lewis know Phillips better than I know Phillips? Confusing, isn't it?)

I don't know Mr. Phillips *as well as Mr. Lewis knows him.*

3. Mrs. Larson *tries* very hard *to get along* with her co-workers. (Does this mean Mrs. Larson *succeeds* or *doesn't succeed* in getting along? There appears to be something hidden behind this statement, but we can't be positive that there's anything lurking there.)

Mrs. Larson *gets along very well* with her co-workers.

If poor word choices can make your writing unclear, imagine what incorrect or confusing sentence structures can do to it. So many things can go wrong with sentences that books have been written entirely about sentence structures.

However, some sentence problems occur more often than others in on-the-job writing. Here are a few prominent ones to watch out for.

### Watch Out for Dangling Sentence Parts

A sentence is supposed to be unified, with all the parts fitting together to make a whole sentence. A "dangling" sentence part means that one part of the sentence doesn't fit with another part. The parts don't make much sense when put together in a whole sentence because one part dangles or isn't connected correctly.

1. As agents for the Midwestern Insurance Company, full payment of claims can be authorized by us.

This sentence literally says that "full payment of claims" are "agents for Midwestern Insurance Company." Does that make any sense? We can see the dangling parts better by taking out a few words between the parts that should be connected.

*As agents* ... full payment of claims ... authorized by *us.*

Now if "us" are the "agents" who are doing the "authorizing," then why are "us" and "agents" at *opposite* ends of the sentence, instead of being *connected*?

*As agents* ... *we* ... authorize full payment of claims.

*As agents* for the Midwestern Insurance Company, *we* can authorize full payment of claims.

2. While visiting your Akron plant, a number of pilfering incidents were discovered by the security team.

This sentence says that "a number of pilfering incidents" did the "visiting." Obviously, that doesn't make sense, but "translating" this sentence accurately is more difficult.

Did the "security team" conduct the visit and also discover the pilfering incidents? Or did *someone else* do the visiting, and the security team just discovered the pilfering while the visit was taking place?

We may *think* we can figure out the answer by studying this sentence carefully. Not this time. Without asking the writer, we can't fully understand this sentence, no matter how hard we try. And, of course, why should the reader have to figure out what the writer is trying to say? It's the writer's responsibility to make sure that the message is clear.

Here's my translation of the sentence. The parts are connected correctly, but have I translated the message accurately? I don't know.

> *While visiting* your Akron plant, *the security team* discovered a number of pilfering incidents.

> 3. After staying up late for two nights, the meeting was difficult for us to stay awake through.

According to this sentence, who stayed up late for two nights? The "meeting" did. Let's try connecting the parts correctly.

> *After staying up late* for two nights, *we* found it difficult to stay awake through the meeting.

In these three examples, the dangling parts could have been avoided if the writers had concentrated on *who* was performing the action in each sentence ("authorizing," "discovering," "staying awake"). The sentence "actor" should appear in the sentence *before* the object *receiving* the action appears.

> (original) ... full payment of claims can be authorized *by us.*
> (better) ... *we* can authorize full payment of claims.

> (original) ... a number of pilfering incidents were discovered *by the security team.*

(better) ... *the security team* discovered a number of pilfering incidents.

(original) ... the meeting was difficult *for us* to stay awake through.
(better) ... *we* found it difficult to stay awake through the meeting.

I'll have more to say about the sentence actor and active/passive sentence structures in Chapter Six.

### Watch Out for Misplaced "Which" and "That" Clauses

Misplaced "which" and "that" clauses also lead to sentence problems. These clauses should be *connected* to the sentence part they *refer to*. They shouldn't be separated.

1. I attended college because I needed a degree to become an accountant in this state in order to get <u>my license, which is my goal in life</u>.

Perhaps the license is this writer's goal in life as the sentence says. However, I think the "which" clause is probably misplaced; it has been separated from the sentence part it actually refers to: "become an accountant."

I attended college because I needed a degree to get licensed in this state <u>as an accountant, which is my goal in life</u>.

2. This preemployment package contains our standard application form and an <u>employee's handbook that you should fill out and return</u>. (The handbook should be filled out and returned?)

This pre-employment package contains an employee's handbook and our standard <u>application form that you should fill out and return</u>.

3. Ms. Simpson has a charge account and often shops

at <u>our store</u>, <u>which she opened last year</u>. (Ms. Simpson opened "our store" last year?)

Ms. Simpson has a <u>charge account</u>, <u>which she opened last year</u>, and often shops at our store.

### Watch Out for "Movable" Words and Phrases

"Movable" words and phrases can be shifted to various parts of the sentence more readily than "which" and "that" clauses can. This flexibility, however, can lead to problems unless these "movable" words and phrases maintain some sort of *connection* to the sentence part they *refer to*.

1. <u>No one</u> is allowed to put anything in this garbage dump <u>except a city employee</u>. (Only city employees can be dumped in the dump?)

<u>No one</u>, <u>except a city employee</u> is allowed to put anything in this garbage dump.

2. To avoid danger of suffocation from <u>this plastic bag</u>, <u>keep</u> away from babies and children. (How will keeping away from babies and children help me avoid danger of suffocation?)

To avoid danger of suffocation, <u>keep</u> <u>this plastic bag</u> away from babies and children.

To avoid danger of suffocation from <u>this plastic bag</u>, <u>keep</u> <u>it</u> away from babies and children.

3. The nurse brought in <u>Robert, Jr.</u>, to see his father <u>bundled up in his baby blanket</u>. (Doesn't Robert's father have his *own* blanket?)

The nurse brought in <u>Robert, Jr.</u>, <u>bundled up in his baby blanket</u>, to see his father.

### Keep Your Sentence Parts Coordinated

"Coordinating" your sentence parts simply means sticking to the sentence pattern you've already set up. The breakdown in coordination usually occurs in sentences that have several parts that are related to one main part.

1. Our new office procedures will help us <u>improve</u> internal controls, <u>eliminating</u> duplication of records, <u>provide</u> better information, and <u>it should facilitate</u> audit review.

This sentence is uncoordinated because the four benefits derived from the new office procedures aren't expressed by using the *same* kind of word to introduce *each* benefit. Each key "benefit" word should follow the example of the *first* benefit word—"improve." This word sets the pattern for the rest of the sentence parts.

Our new office procedures will help us <u>improve</u> internal controls, <u>eliminate</u> duplication of records, <u>provide</u> better information, and <u>facilitate</u> audit review.

Notice how the verbs are now coordinated (often called *parallel*). And starting each sentence part with the same verb form keeps the *rest* of the sentence part coordinated. For example, "it should facilitate audit review" *completely* breaks from the sentence pattern, but "facilitate" brings the part back into the pattern.

Without this coordinated sentence structure, it's possible to misunderstand the message. For instance, "eliminating duplication of records" and "provide better information" and "it should facilitate audit review" could be the benefits *gained from improving* "internal controls." But that's not accurate. "Improved internal controls" are only one of four benefits gained from the "new office procedures." There's a substantial difference in meaning that could result in quite a lot of confusion about what the new office procedures are supposed to accomplish.

2. Five main parts make up the jack: <u>the</u> base, notched shaft, <u>the</u> leverage mechanism, <u>a</u> bumper catch, and handle.

This sentence isn't difficult to understand, but the sentence parts should still be coordinated. Why mix "the" and "a" with items that have no "the" or "a"? It's a careless habit to get into that carries over to more complicated sentences.

Five main parts make up the jack: the base, notched shaft, leverage mechanism, bumper catch, and handle.

3. Last year our company hired 42 accounting majors, 10 majored in finance, and marketing majors made up another 6. (poorly coordinated)

Last year our company hired 42 accounting majors, 10 finance majors, and 6 marketing majors. (better)

Last year our company hired 42 accounting, 10 finance, and 6 marketing majors. (even better)

### Keep the Order of Ideas Straight

Keeping the "order of ideas" straight follows the same guidelines as coordinating the sentence parts, except it's usually not the language that creates problems for the sentence.

1. The company does an import business and was organized in 1975 under the laws of California and is now considering going into exporting.

This kind of writing is just "rambling along" without giving much thought to the sequence of events or order of ideas in the sentence.

Organized in 1975 under California law, the company is an importer and is considering becoming an exporter.

2. The rectangular base is 8 inches long, a molded steel plate, and 6 inches wide. (Why split up the measurements?)

The rectangular base is a molded steel plate, 8 inches long by 6 inches wide. (better)

The rectangular base is an 8-by-6-inch molded steel plate. (even better)

3. Cutting the potatoes into thin strips, the cook adds salt to them after putting them on the grill. (Is this the sequence of events?)

The cook cuts the potatoes into thin strips, places the strips on the grill, and adds some salt.

### Maintain Sentence Logic

Maintaining sentence "logic" is closely related to keeping the order of ideas straight. However, while we can probably unscramble the scrambled order of ideas and put the ideas in the correct sequence, we'll usually have more trouble with "illogical" sentences because we're not absolutely certain what the writer is trying to say.

1. The plans for our new office should be very compact.

The sentence says that the "plans" should be "compact." That doesn't make much sense. On the other hand, I'm *guessing* when I try to make the sentence more logical.

Our new office should be planned so that it's very compact.

2. As soon as they are corrected, these disadvantages will improve our profit margin.

I don't know how "disadvantages" can *improve* anything, especially the "profit margin." But I think I can translate this sentence more accurately.

Correcting these disadvantages will improve our profit margin.

3. This accounting method took as long as five days to implement the program.

How does an "accounting method" implement a program, or anything else for that matter? I always thought people implemented things (or, at least, a committee or task force). And, no, this sentence had nothing to do with computers. I'll try, but I wouldn't bet my translation is accurate.

Using this accounting method, we took five days to implement the program.

Well, now that we've looked at some of the problems on-the-job writers experience in trying to make sure they're understood, take a look at your own writing. See if you can identify any of these problems.

Poor word choices and incorrect or confusing sentences can interfere with your writing effectiveness. The suggestions in this chapter can help you avoid some of the more hazardous roadblocks to making sure your readers fully understand your messages.

*Exercises*
1. Choose the correct word in each sentence:
    a. The miniskirt fad seems to have lost it's/its appeal.
    b. How do you like the design on our new corporate stationary/stationery?
    c. The floral oil painting compliments/complements the new carpeting.
    d. Henry's continual/continuous poor attendance has resulted in his dismissal.
    e. Washington, D.C., is the capital/capitol of the United States.
2. Choose the more *precise* word in each sentence:
    a. For years I've tried to convince/persuade him to hire an additional mechanic.
    b. The promotion committee is apt/liable/likely to pass you over if you don't ask intelligent questions.
    c. We've received a large amount/number of replies to our questionnaire.
    d. Your checking account shows a balance/remainder of $308.96.

e. Our television program has been momentarily/temporarily interrupted.

3. Revise these incorrect sentences:

a. After putting the lid on the jar, the smell of oil was gone.

b. My radio was replaced promptly, but mistakenly charged my account $50.

c. While John cleaned his car windshield, he also checked his tires.

d. The amount of money lost by both the strikers and the employer took a number of years in order to regain it.

e. In keeping with your request there is attached samples of current written guidelines produced by our department.

f. Upon approaching the city, the tallest building could be seen by the visitors.

g. Because of Frank's personal attitude, he's not doing well in his job, which is very hostile.

h. Opening your mail will leave you free later this afternoon in case I need you this morning.

i. Last year our company purchased 378 desks, 110 executive chairs were purchased, and we bought 268 steno chairs, too.

j. If the red light comes on, turn off the engine immediately, which indicates that the engine is overheating.

*Answers to Exercises*

1. a. its ("it's" is the contraction for "it is")

b. stationery ("stationary" means *at rest, not moving*)

c. complements ("compliment" indicates *approval, praise*)

d. continual ("continuous" means *constant, without interruption*)

e. capital ("capitol" refers to a *building*)

2. persuade ("convince" is to get someone to accept some-

thing *mentally*, such as an idea or concept requiring *no action*)

b. likely ("apt" means *suitable, qualified;* "liable" means *accountable*)

c. number ("amount" is used with items that *can't be counted*)

d. balance ("remainder" refers to what's left after performing *subtraction;* bank accounts involve *adding and subtracting*)

e. temporarily ("momentarily" is used with something that will occur in the future: "My boss *will* return momentarily. He *is* temporarily without a car.")

3.    a. After we had put the lid on the jar, the smell of oil disappeared.

b. My radio was replaced promptly, but my account was charged $50 by mistake.

c. After John had cleaned his car windshield, he checked his tires.

d. It took the strikers and the employer a number of years to regain the money they had lost.

e. As you requested, I've attached samples of our department's written guidelines.

f. Upon approaching the city, the visitors could see the tallest building.

g. Because of Frank's personal attitude, which is very hostile, he's not doing well in his job. (Because of Frank's hostile attitude, he's not doing well in his job.)

h. Opening your mail this morning will leave you free later this afternoon in case I need you.

i. Last year our company purchased 378 desks, 110 executive chairs, and 268 steno chairs.

j. If the red light comes on, which indicates that the engine is overheating, turn off the engine immediately.

# CHAPTER FIVE

# Beware of the Jargon Dragon

The "jargon dragon" is constantly on the prowl, confusing people, causing misunderstandings, and interfering with productivity. The dragon has at least two heads: (1) *technical jargon* and (2) *bureaucratic* or *corporate jargon.*

*Technical jargon* is the specialized language of an occupational group. Engineers, accountants, bankers, doctors, lawyers, computer programmers, chemists, geologists, insurance agents, real estate salespeople—almost all occupational groups have technical vocabularies that people in these groups acquire and use.

Technical jargon serves as a shortcut—a quick communication method among people who understand a specialized, occupational vocabulary. If we're writing to people in our occupational groups, we can expect our readers to be familiar with certain specialized terms that the average person wouldn't know. In these writing situations technical jargon can help us communicate our messages effectively.

However, we frequently write to people who aren't in our occupational groups or who don't have the specialized vocabulary that we have. In these situations technical jargon becomes an interference problem because our readers don't understand our technical language.

Our words may be correct, and our sentences may be precise, but we fail as effective writers if our readers can't understand us. It's our job to think about the reader and find a suitable vocabulary to express our messages. Using a suitable, nontechnical vocabulary doesn't mean that we "write down" to the reader. It's more like a *translation* process, except the *writer* does the translating, not the reader.

Take a look at this sentence, for instance:

> The resource control monitor will automatically effectuate a decrease in the intensity of the heat-actuated luminousness of the incandescent lamp.

Unless you happen to belong to the occupational group that produced this particular sentence, you probably aren't sure what the sentence means without looking up some of these words in the dictionary. Even then, I'm not certain that we can capture the *exact* meaning unless we ask someone from inside this company to explain what a "resource control monitor" is.

Well, the "monitor" is a computer. Here's my translation for those of us who suspected that the above message could be expressed in plain English:

> The computer will automatically turn down the light.

I believe most of us—if we think about our readers—can see why such technical jargon is inappropriate for readers outside our occupational groups. Actually, words such as "effectuated," "heat-actuated," and "luminousness" aren't necessary for technical readers either. These words are examples of "puffed up" or "inflated" language, which I'll discuss in more detail for the rest of this chapter.

The jargon dragon's other head, *bureaucratic* or *corporate jargon*, is more difficult to avoid because it sneaks up on us. Other names for this type of jargon are *gobbledygook*, *doublespeak*, *pretentious*, *pompous*, *puffed-up*, or *inflated* writing. I'll just call it *bureaucratic* jargon.

Bureaucratic jargon *inflates* the language beyond what is necessary to put the message across effectively. This type of jargon uses "big" words (or uncommon words) instead of "small" words (or more common words). In addition, bureaucratic jargon sometimes uses complicated, involved sentences instead of straightforward, easy-to-understand sentences.

Here's a typical example of bureaucratic jargon:

> It is the policy of this company to provide the proper employment equipment to enable each employee to participate in the interoffice and intraoffice activities necessitated by the proper discharge of his or her employment-related responsibilities. (37 words)

I contend that no eighteen-year-old employee just starting his or her "employment-related responsibilities" (also known as "work") would ever dream of writing such a sentence. But let our eighteen-year-old work for a few years (maybe months?) in an organization where he or she is exposed to a steady diet of letters, memos, and reports, and gradually, our aging eighteen-year-old's language will become "fatter," covering up most of the muscle and sinew with well-inflated, flabby words and sentences.

Why does the jargon dragon have such an easy time puffing up our language? I have a theory. From the time we can talk and read, we're encouraged to develop our vocabulary (learn five new words a day; use them in sentences; then you've mastered them, etc.). We're impressed by "big" words because people using these words are "educated."

This learning process is fine, since we need to improve our vocabulary to be able to understand newspapers, books, speeches, ideas, etc. However, this process actually works *against* us when we start writing on the job because we think that sounding "educated" means using more complicated language.

The purpose of on-the-job writing is to *communicate* messages to our readers, not to display vocabulary achievements. Readers want *information* from letters, memos, and reports. They don't want an education in language usage. The best words to use are the simplest words, the easiest ones to understand, the words we use in our everyday speech.

Certainly, we should use words that *sound* like us. Dartmouth Professor David Lambuth struck at the heart of the jargon dragon in 1923 when he wrote: "Although there is much mistaken opinion to the contrary, literary English does not demand a stiff, stilted Latinistic vocabulary. It demands the simplest words, the most familiar words, the most concrete words consistent with accurate expression and good everyday usage."

Now take another look at our "company policy" example. Read the sentence aloud. Does it *sound* like someone would actually *say* this to anyone? I'm not making a pitch for you to write *exactly* the way you speak (we usually need to straighten up our writing a little bit). But you should avoid bureaucratic jargon as much as possible. Try to sound "natural" (more about this point in the chapter on "tone").

Here's a revised "company policy" sentence that comes closer to a natural expression. It's also more concise and easier to understand.

Our company will provide you with the necessary tools to do your job. (13 words)

The ability to put across our ideas in straightforward, concrete language shows how well we've mastered our language. Using bureaucratic jargon doesn't make the writer more "educated." In fact, writers who rely on this type of jargon don't write well at all. The language *looks* impressive, but frequently the content lacks substance. In such cases, the writer is hiding behind the language to disguise muddled thinking or poorly thought out ideas.

Or perhaps the writer simply doesn't want to take the time to write in plain English. Once we get into the jargon habit, it's much easier to call the jargon dragon from its cave.

But let's put things into perspective. All of us have our favorite jargon words and phrases. It's not the *occasional* use of jargon that leads to inflated, pretentious writing. Most poor writing results from *overusing* jargon, making it the *dominant* part of the writing style. The jargon habit becomes ingrained in the writing style over a period of time (I'll discuss the "wordiness habit" in the next chapter).

The dragon sneaks up on us and "captures" our writing. We're usually not aware that our writing is the dragon's prisoner unless we begin to look at our writing from a critical point of view.

Some writing experts consider jargon the number-one interference problem in the writing process. There are certainly many good reasons for ranking it at or near the top. Here are just a few:

1. Jargon usually makes messages unnecessarily complicated when, in fact, many messages are quite simple if expressed in plain English (see the jargon examples used in this chapter).

2. Readers are busy, too. Many readers won't take the time necessary to figure out *exactly* what the message says. *Partial* understanding leads to misunderstandings.

3. Readers also have egos. Many people are embarrassed to admit they didn't understand something, particularly if they feel that it's something they should have understood. Consequently, they may say nothing, *even though* the message wasn't understood. The jargon dragon intimidates them.

4. Jargon writers often use words, phrases, or sentences that *look* impressive but that are inappropriate or incorrect. Sometimes the language *sounds* pretty good ("sophisticated," "educated," etc.), but the message can't be translated with any degree of accuracy.

5. Jargon writers frequently defend their writing by saying "everyone around here understands this type of writing," or "if you worked here, you would know what I mean," etc. Time and time again this defensive wall has crumbled when people *in the same organization* have been put on the spot by being asked to explain what their jargon-laden letters, memos, and reports meant. I've been in some sessions in which no two people from the same section could agree upon what their own written documents meant.

Here are some ideas to help you avoid the jargon dragon.

### *Avoid Overusing "Inflated" Words*

Try to use words that most people use and understand, instead of "inflating" your language. Don't get carried away, of course. If you use certain inflated words when you *speak*, and these words *sound* like you, by all means use them in your written communication. On the other hand, if you use inflated words only *occasionally* when you speak, avoid putting these occasional words together in the same sentence just to puff up your language. Either avoid using inflated words entirely or use them sparingly.

| *Instead of writing ...* | *Why not write ...* |
| --- | --- |
| ascertain | find out |
| compensation | pay |
| conglomeration | mixture |
| disseminate | spread |
| endeavor | try |
| incombustible | fireproof |
| modification | change |
| ramification | consequence |
| transmit | send |
| vacillate | waver |

The list of such words is very long, but I think you get the idea. Now look at what happens when these words are strung together in sentences.

1. I'll *endeavor* to *ascertain* whether the date of the delivery is subject to *modification*.

I'll try to find out whether the shipment date can be changed.

2. This *incombustible* material will slow down the *dissemination* of flames.

This fireproof material will slow down the spread of flames.

3. He keeps *vacillating* about what the *ramifications* will be if he *undercompensates* his employees.

He keeps wavering about what the consequences will be if he underpays his employees.

### Use Common Words Instead of Uncommon Words

Most of us use certain words more often than others. "Common" words are words that the average person knows and uses frequently in everyday speech. It's true that our reading vocabularies are usually much larger than our speaking vocabularies, but reading vocabularies vary considerably among people, depending upon what kind of reading they do. Since we're supposed to *communicate* with our readers, we're better off sticking to words that fall within the average person's vocabulary.

| Instead of writing ... | Why not write ... |
| --- | --- |
| ameliorate | improve |
| antithesis | opposite |
| contiguous | near |
| elucidate | clarify |
| expunge | wipe out |
| innocuous | harmless |
| obviate | prevent |
| orifice | opening |
| quadrilateral | four-sided |
| veracious | true |

This list can become quite long also. Here are some sentences using a few of these words. Could the reader understand the sentences without looking up the words in a dictionary? How many readers would take the time?

1. Her criticism of our company's failure to *ameliorate*

its profits was the *antithesis* of her usually *innocuous* statements.

Her criticism of our company's failure to improve its profits was the opposite of her usually harmless statements.

2. Take precautions to *obviate* the *orifice* from enlarging.

Take precautions to prevent the opening from enlarging.

3. I realize that *elucidating* my comments won't *expunge* the confusion I've caused.

I realize that clarifying my comments won't wipe out the confusion I've caused.

### Avoid Overusing Jargon Phrases

Jargon phrases are phrases that have been used so much that they've become clichés. Such phrases are usually wordy, awkward, and more complicated than necessary to get the point across.

| *Instead of writing ...* | *Why not write...* |
| --- | --- |
| demonstrates that there is | shows |
| during such time as | while |
| hold in abeyance | wait, hold |
| if the developments are such that | if |
| in consideration of the fact that | because |
| make an approximation as to how | estimate |
| reduced to basic essentials | simplified |
| the purpose of this report is to show | this report shows |
| there is no question that | unquestionably |
| would seem to suggest | suggests |

Recognize any of your favorites? I've found a couple of mine in this batch. This list can go on and on. Some people become quite adept at writing this way.

1. *The purpose of this report is to demonstrate that there is* a need *to make an approximation as to how* much we can budget for leasing automobiles next year.

This reports shows we need to estimate next year's automobile leasing budget.

2. *In consideration of the fact that* you've made this month's payment, we'll *hold* our court action *in abeyance.*

Because you've made this month's payment, we'll hold up our court action.

3. *During such time as* we are waiting for economic conditions to improve, *if the developments are such that* you see an attractive investment, please notify us.

While we're waiting for economic conditions to improve, if you see an attractive investment, please notify us.

### Avoid Using Vague Jargon

Most of the jargon we've looked at so far can be translated if we want to take the time and effort to work our way through it. "Vague" jargon presents another problem. This type of jargon uses words and phrases that have many different meanings, depending on the contexts of the messages. Unfortunately, even in the proper context, it's often difficult (if not impossible) to understand what some of this jargon means. Here are some words that should be used very cautiously because it's hard to pin down what they mean.

| | |
|---|---|
| facilitate | parameters |
| feasibility | polarize |
| finalization | priortize |
| impact | proximity |
| input | totality |
| interface | ultimate |
| manifest | utilization |
| output | viable |

I won't even try to translate these sentences, but I think you'll see how these words can get out of hand, especially when they're combined with each other or with other vague words.

1. It's necessary for us to *priortize* our *interface* capabilities in order to determine the operational *impact* of our policy modification standards.

2. Our operational malfeasance monitor is in its *finalization* stage, which should allow us the *feasibility* of *facilitating* consideration of most of the *viable parameters.*

3. The *proximity* of the *input* to the *output* considerations gives us a solid picture of the *ultimate utilization* of our manufacturing operation in its *totality.*

As on-the-job writers, we must be constantly aware of the jargon dragon's power to infiltrate our writing. Often this infiltration occurs so slowly that the dragon takes over our writing without our being consciously aware of the "capture." It's tough to shake the dragon because we hate to give up rather comfortable writing habits.

If you haven't let the dragon out of its cave yet—good. Let it sleep.

*Exercises*

1. Substitute "everyday" words for these "inflated" words.

beneficial _____

cognizant _____

commence _____

conjecture _____

divest _____

encounter _____

illuminate _____

indeterminate _____
indubitably _____
ineffectual _____
necessitate _____
paramount _____
problematical _____
reproduction _____
voluminous _____

2. Substitute more "common" words for these "uncommon" words.

actuate _____
circuitous _____
commodious _____
configuration _____
inundate _____
nebulous _____
oblique _____
promulgate _____
protuberance _____
quiescent _____
requisite _____
succor _____
supersede _____
undulations _____
veracity _____

3. Substitute other words for these jargon phrases.

according to the law _____
as a matter of fact _____
beyond a shadow of a doubt _____
by way of illustration _____
conditions that exist _____
consensus of opinion _____
for the purpose of _____
for the reason that _____
in accordance with _____

leaving out of consideration _____
of no mean ability _____
on the occasion of _____
pursuant to _____
subject of a controversial nature _____
until such time as _____

*Answers to Exercises*

1. beneficial  (helpful)
   cognizant  (aware)
   commence  (start, begin)
   conjecture  (guess)
   divest  (free)
   encounter  (meet)
   illuminate  (clarify, explain, light up)
   indeterminate  (vague)
   indubitably  (doubtless)
   ineffectual  (useless, unsuccessful)
   necessitate  (require)
   paramount  (main, chief)
   problematical  (doubtful, uncertain)
   reproduction  (copy)
   voluminous  (large, bulk)

2. actuate  (move)
   circuitous  (indirect, roundabout)
   commodious  (roomy, spacious)
   configuration  (contour, shape)
   inundate  (overwhelm, flood)
   nebulous  (vague)
   oblique  (slanting)
   promulgate  (announce, make known, declare)
   protuberance  (bulge)
   quiescent  (quiet, still)
   requisite  (needed, required)
   succor  (help)
   supersede  (replace)

undulations (waves)
veracity (truth)

3. according to the law  (legally)
   as a matter of fact  (in fact)
   beyond a shadow of a doubt  (doubtless, undoubtedly)
   by way of illustration  (for example, for instance)
   conditions that exist  (conditions)
   consensus of opinion  (consensus)
   for the purpose of  (for, to)
   for the reason that  (because, since)
   in accordance with  (by, under)
   leaving out of consideration  (disregarding)
   of no mean ability  (capable, qualified)
   on the occasion of  (when)
   pursuant to  (following)
   subject of a controversial nature  (controversial subject)
   until such time as  (until)

# CHAPTER SIX

---

# Write Concisely

---

"Wordiness" is a major problem that many writers constantly struggle to overcome. It's much easier to write "verbosely" instead of "concisely" because writing concisely forces us to be more precise in the way we express our ideas.

Concise writing means using fewer words to express your message, without changing the meaning or ignoring sound grammatical principals. Simply making your sentences less wordy can produce writing that allows your reader to understand your message more quickly and easily.

Why is concise writing important? Imagine reading ten memos a day (some people read even more). Let's say that each memo contains 1,500 words; however, the information could have been expressed in only 500 words. Instead of reading 5,000 words, you must read 15,000 words to obtain the *same information.*

*Habitual* wordiness wastes everyone's time—the writer's, the typist's, and the reader's. If we *always* use more words than are necessary, we're interfering with the productivity of everyone who reads our letters, memos, and reports.

Here are some wordy sentences that should have been revised:

> We request that the portion of the confidential application that is labeled as confidential be treated as confidential in view of the fact that the information contained therein includes confidential information. (31 words)

> I can only state my personal opinion, which is based upon observations made by me personally, which

is that twelve-hour workdays tend to be too long for most workers to be at their peak, which is one of the reasons that they are not performing at their peak efficiency. (50 words)

It's easy to ramble on this way sentence after sentence, paragraph after paragraph, page after page, until the wirter finally succeeds in boring, irritating, or confusing the reader. Such writing shows a lack of discipline on the writer's part because the writer doesn't try to *control* the language—it's on automatic pilot.

A more disciplined writer might start out with something like this example:

> After reviewing all of the reasons you give for the causes of all of our problems with delinquent accounts, I find that your analysis is correct. (26 words)

But by pruning the excess verbiage, the writer can quickly reduce the sentence to its *essential* parts:

> Your delinquent account analysis is correct. (6 words)

Although it's difficult to be arbitrary about sentence length, if your sentences *average* more than 18–21 words, you're probably being too wordy. To determine whether your writing is too wordy, count the words in ten sentences; then divide by 10 to obtain your average sentence length. For example, the first ten sentences of this chapter average 16.3 words in length (12 + 25 + 19 + 22 + 5 + 11 + 19 + 15 + 12 + 23 = 163 ÷ 10 = 16.3).

We're all too wordy sometimes. It's not the *occasional* use of wordy phrases or sentences that causes us to lose control over our writing. We're looking for wordiness that occurs repeatedly, until it becomes our writing style without our giving it much thought. The writers who wrote the wordy, involved sentences used as examples at the start of this chapter didn't suddenly change their styles for the rest of their documents. The same wordy patterns continued.

Fortunately, the wordiness habit can be controlled by identifying your wordy patterns and applying some techniques to change those patterns, until you acquire the "conciseness" habit.

Here are some ideas that can help you write more concisely.

### Shorten Wordy Phrases and Eliminate Unnecessary Ones

Many times we can start chopping out extra words by simply letting one or two words perform the work of several words.

1. We've received your check in the amount of $57.98 payable to the order of James Smith.

We've received your check in the amount of $57.98 payable to the order of James Smith.
*(for, with "in the amount of" and "the order of" struck out)*

2. Please call me in the very near future.

Please call me in the very near future.
*(soon, with "in the very near future" struck out)*

3. Due to the fact that you didn't pay your bill, we canceled your service.

Due to the fact that you didn't pay your bill, we canceled your service.
*(Because, with "Due to the fact that" struck out)*

### Eliminate Hackneyed, Worn-out Introductions to Sentences

We frequently fall into the habit of "warming up" before we reveal the true content of our sentences. Warming up with trite, "automatic pilot" sentence introductions just adds many unnecessary words to our sentences. Such phrases also add nothing to our message, although we sometimes try to convince ourselves that all those words couldn't be completely useless. They are.

1. I would like to take this opportunity to thank you for your donation.

~~I would like to take this opportunity to~~ Thank you for your donation.

2. Please be advised that we will send your check next week.

~~Please be advised that~~ We will send your check next week.

3. It has come to my attention that we need to examine the budget closely.

~~It has come to my attention that~~ We need to examine the budget closely.

## Avoid Using Redundant Words

Using another word that means almost the same thing as the word we've just written is an easy habit to acquire and often difficult to notice in our writing. But it results in a form of communication overkill that makes writing unnecessarily wordy.

1. Please give me a full and complete report.

Please give me a ~~full and~~ complete report.

2. We first began this project last October.

We ~~first~~ began this project last October.

3. Please give my recommendation your prompt and immediate attention.

Please give my recommendation your ~~prompt and~~ immediate attention.

## Avoid Overuse of "Dummy" Subjects

Although starting sentences with "dummy" subjects ("there is," "it is," etc.) can be an effective way to get into your sentences, the "dummy" subject usually results in longer sentences. Overusing this sentence pattern will make your writing wordy and your verbs predominantly passive (is, has, etc.).

1. It has been determined by the committee that next year's company picnic will cost too much.

~~It has been determined by~~ The committee <sub>determined</sub> that next year's company picnic will cost too much.

2. There are many things that will prevent us from expanding our operation until next year.

~~There are~~ Many things ~~that~~ will prevent us from expanding our operation until next year.

3. It is necessary for us to begin planning the annual report layout.

~~It is necessary for us to~~ <sup>We should</sup> begin planning the annual report layout.

### *Avoid Overuse of "Be" Verb Forms*

The verb "*be*" is probably the most valuable verb in our language. It's also the most overworked verb. We use it so often that we forget how passive the verb is. "Be" expresses no action and shouldn't substitute for action verbs. Relying on "be" verb forms can also lead to wordy sentences because the verb usually needs the help of other verb forms and prepositional phrases to complete an action.

1. We are of the belief that this report is inaccurate.

We ~~are of the belief that~~ <sup>believe</sup> this report is inaccurate.

2. Tomorrow we are going to recommend her for promotion.

Tomorrow we ~~are going to~~ <sup>will</sup> recommend her for promotion.

3. We are always in need of additional people to help us.

We ~~are~~ always ~~in~~ need ~~of~~ additional people to help us.

### Place the Sentence Actor Near the Beginning of the Sentence

The "sentence actor" performs the action of the sentence. The "sentence object" receives the action. In our language the shortest, most direct way to express action is to place the sentence actor near the beginning of the sentence, not at the end. Placing the sentence actor up front also allows you to use *strong, active verbs* and avoid repetition of the prepositional phrase starting with "by."

Notice the *repetitive, passive verb patterns* in the first sentences of each pair below. Understanding how to make your sentences *active* instead of *passive* will make you a much more powerful writer because your written communication will be more concise, more direct, and appear more decisive.

1. The special report ⟨ was prepared by ⟩ the <u>task force</u> (sentence actor).

The <u>task force</u> ⟨ prepared ⟩ the special report.

2. We ⟨ have been requested by ⟩ the <u>Richmond Office</u> (sentence actor) to change our current system.

The <u>Richmond Office</u> ⟨ requested ⟩ us to change our current system.

3. It ⟨ has been decided by ⟩ our <u>supervisor</u> (sentence actor) that we will work overtime this week.

Our <u>supervisor</u> ⟨ decided ⟩ that we will work overtime this week.

### Avoid Overusing the Preposition "Of"

The trouble with prepositions is that they introduce prepositional phrases, which can lead to all sorts of wordiness problems and involved, confusing sentences. The preposition "*of*" is the workhorse in on-the-job writing, and like most workhorses in our language, it gets overused. It's certainly my favorite preposition, as you've probably noticed if you've scanned my sentences even casually. Other prepositions often overused include "*in,*" "*on,*" "*to,*" and "*for*"; but "*of*" leads the pack.

Here are some "*of*" uses that can easily be avoided, thus producing more concise sentences.

1. The file of John reflected some problem of work that took place in November of 1978.

~~The file of John~~ John's file reflected some ~~problem of work~~ problem work that took place in November ~~of~~ 1978.

2. Notification of the family of the proper claim procedures should occur before the 9th of April.

~~Notification of~~ Notify the family of the proper claim procedures ~~should occur~~ before ~~the 9th of~~ April 9.

3. I've determined most of the reasons for many of the problems we're experiencing.

I've determined most ~~of the~~ reasons for many ~~of the~~ problems we're experiencing.

### Combine Related Sentence Elements

Sometimes we drag out our message because we don't see the relationship between two or more sentences. In a sense we express one idea in one sentence and then end the sentence. Then we express another idea in the next sentence and stop again. Many times, however, the ideas in the *separate* sentences are closely related and could easily be combined into one sentence, which will usually be more concise.

1. We have your letter of June 15 asking how to transfer ownership of your stock certificates. In order to make

the transfer, it will be necessary for you to sign the enclosed form. (33 words)

To transfer ownership of the stock certificates mentioned in your June 15 letter, please sign the enclosed form. (18 words)

2. There are three ways to handle this problem. The first way is to ignore it. The second way is to refer it to someone else. The third way is to solve it. (32 words)

There are three ways to handle this problem: ignore it, refer it to someone else, or solve it. (18 words)

3. On September 21 we sent you a letter about your policy. In that letter we informed you that your policy had lapsed. The reason the policy had lapsed was that you did not pay the quarterly premium. This premium was due on June 30. (44 words)

Our September 21 letter informed you that your policy had lapsed because you didn't pay the June 30 quarterly premium. (20 words)

In the examples used above, it's true the original writers used short sentences that averaged less than our 18–21 average sentence guideline. But the overall effect is the same; they are using too many words to express their ideas. Example 3 averages only 11 words per sentence but still takes 44 words overall to do the job of 20 words. Writer 3 continued writing the rest of the letter the same wordy way, thus making it *over twice* as long as it needed to be.

### Leave Out Unnecessary Details
Perhaps because we enjoy reading stories and telling stories, we often try to cram too much *extra* information into our sentences. It's natural to want to relate "everything that happened" or "how I went about finding out this information," but on-the-job writing should stress the *essential* information *the reader needs* to understand the situation.

Here are some examples of "storytelling" writing and suggested revisions.

1. If you hadn't reported the loss so promptly, we would be unable to do anything for you; however, in your case, we are glad to tell you that we can help you. (32 words)

Because you reported the loss promptly, we will be able to help you. (13 words)

2. I telephoned your office on Monday, September 29, and talked to Sue, and she indicated to me that you were still using the blank 1580 form in some cases. (29 words)

On September 29, Sue told me you were still using the blank 1580. (13 words)

3. When I contacted Dr. Miller on August 8, I was informed by him that Mr. Lewis was still in the hospital, and Dr. Miller also told me that Mr. Lewis probably wouldn't be released from the hospital until early September. (40 words)

On August 8, Dr. Miller told me Mr. Lewis was in the hospital and probably wouldn't be released until early September. (21 words)

These writers forgot that their readers want to know *what they found out,* not the whole story about how they telephoned offices, talked to people, who then gave them some information, etc.

You can use these ideas to (1) *identify* wordiness patterns in your writing and then (2) *apply* some of the techniques to cut down on your wordy phrases, sentences, and paragraphs. Go through some samples of your writing; circle or mark wordy phrases and sentences. See if you can identify any patterns that look similar to the ones I've discussed in this chapter. If you identify more than one problem area, try to work on only one problem at a time, until you've gained control over that particular habit. Then go on to the next one.

*Exercises*

1. These phrases appear in on-the-job writing constantly. Each phrase performs a job that one word could do. Try to substitute *one word* for each phrase.

in the amount of _____
in the neighborhood of _____
with reference to _____
due to the fact that _____
enclosed please find _____
at the earliest possible date _____
at the present time _____
during the period from _____
in the immediate future _____
in order to _____
by means of _____
despite the fact that _____
during the course of _____
during the time that _____
from time to time _____
in many instances _____
in the normal course of procedure _____
it is apparent that _____
it is obvious that _____
tends to support _____

2. Rewrite these sentences by changing them from passive to active sentence patterns.

a. The banquet facilities were provided by the hotel management.

b. Our family was notified about John's condition by Dr. Smothers.

c. My automobile repair estimate was prepared by the service manager.

    d. The nails were driven into the wood by the carpenter.

    e. The cows were milked by the farmer this morning.

3. Combine the related sentence elements into one sentence.

    a. Mrs. Rogers built a fence last week. The fence is made of wood. (13 words)

    b. The management of this company has tried hard to cut down the rate of absenteeism. It has been very difficult to do this because many of the employees don't like their jobs. (32 words)

    c. Susan applied for a position with the Trevor Manufacturing Company. She applied two weeks ago. An accounting position was open and Susan was interested in it. (26 words)

    d. A drill press is a machine for drilling holes in wood or metal. It is a valuable machine shop tool that has a lot of versatility. It's also dangerous when not operated properly. (33 words)

    e. Business executives have recognized the need for effective written communication. They recognized this need many years ago. Now more and more of them are beginning to do something about it by polishing up their skills. (35 words)

4. Using your pen or pencil, edit this memo by crossing out unnecessary words and phrases and combining related ideas.

    These dresses are the latest in design and should be good sales items if they are promoted properly. I suggest that these dresses be advertised in the local newspapers and magazines in order to get maximum exposure for these items. These dresses should be prominently displayed in your section to gain maximum customer appeal for the dresses. You should brief your staff regarding the best way to sell these dresses.

5. Revise the following sentences to make them more concise. Try not to cut out the *essential content* of the message. Your revised sentences should be *grammatically sound*, not pieces or fragments. We'll start with a couple of sentences used earlier in this chapter.

a. We request that the portion of the confidential application that is labeled as confidential be treated as confidential in view of the fact that the information contained therein includes confidential information. (31 words)

b. I can only state my personal opinion, which is based upon observations made by me personally, which is that twelve-hour workdays tend to be too long for most workers to be at their peak, which is one of the reasons that they are not performing at their peak efficiency. (50 words)

c. Effective July 1 and thereafter, checks written in the amount of one thousand dollars and over one thousand dollars must be cosigned by the controller of our company in addition to the signature of the manager of the accounts payable department of our company. (44 words)

d. The items that were ordered by you are going to be shipped by us on March 31. (17 words; it's short, but wordy)

e. Please find enclosed our request that your recommendation be conveyed to this office, in writing, in the immediate future. (19 words; not too long, just wordy)

*Answers to Exercises*
1. in the amount of (for)
   in the neighborhood of (about, approximately)
   with reference to (about)
   due to the fact that (because)
   enclosed please find (enclosed)

at the earliest possible date (soon, quickly, immediately)

at the present time (now, presently, currently)

during the period from (from, between)

in the immediate future (soon, quickly, immediately)

in order to (to)

by means of (by)

despite the fact that (though)

during the course of (during)

during the time that (when, while)

from time to time (occasionally)

in many instances (often)

in the normal course of procedure (normally, usually)

it is apparent that (apparently)

it is obvious that (obviously)

tends to support (supports)

2. a. The hotel management provided the banquet facilities.

   b. Dr. Smothers notified our family about John's condition.

   c. The service manager prepared my automobile repair estimate.

   d. The carpenter drove the nails into the wood.

   e. The farmer milked the cows this morning.

3. a. Mrs. Rogers built a wooden fence last week. (8 words)

   b. Management has had a difficult time cutting the absenteeism rate because many employees don't like their jobs. (17 words)

   c. Two weeks ago Susan applied for an accounting position with the Trevor Manufacturing Company. (14 words)

d. A drill press is a versatile machine shop tool for drilling holes in wood or metal, but it's dangerous when not operated properly. (23 words)

e. Years ago business executives recognized the need for effective written communication; now more of them are polishing their skills. (19 words)

4. These dresses are the latest ~~in design~~ and should be good sales items if ~~they are~~ promoted properly. I suggest that ~~these dresses be~~ advertised ~~in the local newspapers~~

you them locally,

~~and magazines in order to get maximum exposure for these items. These dresses should be prominently~~ dis-
~~played in your section to gain maximum customer-~~
them prominently,
~~appeal for the dresses. You should~~ brief your staff
and
~~regarding~~ the best way to sell ~~these dresses.~~ (35 words)
on them.

These dresses are the latest and should be good sales items if promoted properly. I suggest that you advertise them locally, display them prominently, and brief your staff on the best way to sell them. (35 words)

5. a. Please respect the confidential portion of this application. (8 words)

b. I've observed that twelve-hour workdays are too long for most workers to perform at peak efficiency. (17 words)

c. Effective July 1, checks $1,000 and over must be cosigned by our company controller and accounts payable manager. (18 words)

d. Your order will be shipped March 31. (7 words)

e. Please send your written recommendations to me immediately. (8 words)

# CHAPTER SEVEN

# Adopt an Appropriate Tone

The "tone" of your writing goes beyond the content of your message: it's how your message *sounds* to the reader. In Chapter Three we saw how important it is to show an awareness of your reader while at the same time satisfying your aims. We looked at the "you approach" to writing. This approach is one way to control the tone of your message, but there are several other ways, too.

Controlling the tone doesn't change the content of your message, but it can influence how your reader *responds* or *reacts* to your message. The *way* we say something sometimes affects our readers more strongly than *what* we say. Think how disturbing it is for someone to resist your ideas simply because he or she didn't like the tone of your message. Inappropriate tone can create significant interference problems.

As listeners, we can tell from the tone of a person's voice whether that person is upset, angry, pleasant, sarcastic, or whatever. Words on paper "speak" to us in much the same way. The tone of a letter, memo, or report can be positive, negative, neutral, formal, informal, conversational, pleasant, sarcastic, condescending, optimistic, pessimistic, or just about anything else. Sometimes several of these ingredients are combined in the same document.

A document's tone allows us to draw a mental picture of the writer. We don't always think about the writer *consciously,* but we can almost "see" the person (or determine the person's frame of mind or attitude) just by "listening" to the material.

Let's take a look at some examples. What kind of tone comes across to you in these messages?

1. Dear Steve:

Thanks so much for your very gracious invitation to First Security's luncheon on January 8, at the Banker's Club in Phillipsburg.

I'm really disappointed I can't be present for your luncheon because I had planned to attend this year. As you know, however, we're conducting a series of workshops on banking regulations during the next two weeks. I'm scheduled to be in Trevorville on the date of your get-together.

Phil Travis will be there to represent us, though. Phil joined our staff last year and calls on banks in your state. He's looking forward to meeting you and other members of your staff.

I'll phone Mrs. Rogers to confirm Phil's attendance, but I wanted you to know how sorry I am that I'll miss seeing all of you.

2.   TO: All Department Heads
     SUBJECT: New Policy Orientation Meeting

There will be a meeting in my office on Tuesday, March 21, at 1 P.M. I expect all of you to be there and to bring your copies of my January 25 memo about the new policies we were supposed to implement by February 15.

I've been forced to call this meeting because a few of you obviously don't understand what some of our new policies are. You'll understand them much better after the meeting.

It will be good to see all of you again. We should have a productive meeting.

3.   TO: All Dept. 8962 Employees
     SUBJECT: Cleaning Requirements

This memorandum represents an attempt to inform all department employees about the desirability of cleaning around their work stations before they retire from work for the evening. It has been noticed by senior management personnel who have toured the employee areas that some employees in certain determined areas have failed to observe standard cleanliness procedures around their machines.

Although the numbers of employees committing the most flagrant abuses of the cleaning requirements are minimal, it is feasible that their malfeasance may infect the rest of the employee population.

Hence, the necessity of writing this memorandum to remind all of you of your cleanliness responsibilities and the cleanliness procedures, which must be observed by all concerned.

Example 1 ("Dear Steve" letter) expresses a negative message in an upbeat way. The writer seems to be genuinely sorry to miss the luncheon. The writer also shows concern for the reader's aims by saying that Phil Travis will "represent us." The tone is friendly, sincere, personal, and positive.

The writer achieves a "personal" tone by using pronouns (I, you, he, we) frequently. In addition, notice the use of contractions (I'm, I'll, we're, he's). Contractions can make our writing sound informal, almost as if we're *speaking* directly to the reader. Even though the writer uses "I" quite a few times, the "you approach" still comes across ("your luncheon," "you know," "your get-together," "meeting you," "your staff," "seeing all of you").

In fact, alternating between "I" and "you" pronouns makes the tone sound even more personal because there seems to be some sort of give-and-take going on between the writer and reader.

But a "personal" tone doesn't always produce a "friendly," "sincere," and "positive" letter. The writer achieves an upbeat tone by using *positive* reasons for saying "no." With the exception of the one piece of negative information that has to be put across ("I'm really disappointed I can't be present"), the writer stresses *positive* actions throughout the letter ("I had planned to attend," "we're conducting," "I'm scheduled to be," "Phil Travis will be there," "He's looking forward to," "I'll phone Mrs. Rogers," "I wanted you to know," "I'll miss seeing ... you").

It would have been easy to decline this luncheon invitation in a very negative way ("I regret that I cannot attend the luncheon because my schedule does not permit it as I am obligated to ... " etc.). This writer, however, decided to take a more positive approach and *controlled* the tone by stressing *positive* words, phrases, and actions. The message content remains the same, of course, whether it's expressed negatively or positively: the writer turned down the invitation.

In this case the writer adopted an appropriate tone for the situation.

Example 2 ("All Department Heads" memo) has a dictatorial tone in the first two paragraphs ("There *will* be," "I *expect* all of you"). There's also an element of sarcasm present ("we were *supposed* to implement," "a few of you *obviously* don't understand"). Notice the threatening sentence: "You'll understand them *much* better *after* the meeting." This meeting sounds as if it 's going to be somewhat uncomfortable for the department heads.

The writer's irritation or anger has creeped into the tone of the memo. If the writer had *wanted* the memo to sound "upset," then the writer succeeded in controlling the tone. We might question the writer's judgment in sending such a memo to *all* department heads when only a *few* don't understand. If I were one of the department heads who *did* understand, I think the memo's tone might ruffle my feathers unnecessarily because I received the same memo as the "dumb" ones. Maybe I'm too sensitive?

However, the memo's last paragraph shows that the writer *wasn't* controlling the tone. After those first two paragraphs, do we really believe the writer is sincere in saying, "It will be good to see all of you again"? That statement sounds phony; it certainly doesn't belong with the rest of this memo. I'm not sure I believe the writer is genuinely concerned about having "a productive meeting."

Example 3 ("All Dept. 8962 Employees" memo) also has sarcastic elements in it, but overall the tone is pretentious and pompous. The tone sounds aloof because the writer uses inflated words and phrases (bureaucratic jargon) that "elevate" the language. Actually, the message is quite simple: Clean around your machines before you leave.

Notice some of the inflated wording that contributes to this elevated tone:

| *Inflated Wording* | *Plain English* |
| --- | --- |
| "retire from work for the evening" | quit work for the day |
| "senior management personnel" | management, supervisors |
| "toured the employee areas" | walked through the shop |
| "failed to observe standard cleanliness procedures" | didn't clean up |

The writer really gets carried away in paragraph two. The employees aren't just failing to clean up, they're committing "flagrant abuses" and their "malfeasance may *infect* the rest of the employee population." It sounds like a disease of some sort is loose in the shop.

Words such as "flagrant," "abuses," and "malfeasance" aren't appropriate for this type of memo because they exaggerate what's taking place in the shop. If things were actually this bad, the "minimal" numbers of employees committing the "abuses" would probably be disciplined or fired, instead of just being *reminded* to observe the cleaning rules.

It's hard to see how this kind of inflated writing can be appropriate in any on-the-job situation. Often, however, people who write this way aren't aware of what their writing *sounds* like. They can see the words, but they can't *hear* them.

Adopting an appropriate tone for the situation means thinking about *how* you express your message as well as *what* your message says. You can ignore your tone—some on-the-job writers would like to believe that tone isn't important—but your reader won't ignore it. You can *control* your tone, but you can't eliminate it. All written documents have tone.

Controlling your tone involves selecting words and phrases that will help you project the attitude and self-image you *want your reader to see* and that will help you *communicate* with your reader *more effectively.*

Here are some suggestions to help you adopt an appropriate tone.

### Use a Personal Tone

I touched on this point in Chapter Three when I discussed using the pronoun "you" to replace "impersonal" writing. Although we're usually representing our organizations, we should remember that *people* write and read letters, memos, and reports; organizations don't. Using a personal tone means putting a *person*, preferably yourself, into the message.

1. *It* is suggested that *this department* be supplied with the latest figures. (impersonal)

*I* suggest that *you* send *us* the latest figures. (personal)

2. *There* is a memorandum enclosed. (impersonal)

*I'm* enclosing a memorandum. (personal)

3. The *Williams Tire Company* stands behind *its* products and knows *its customers* appreciate *its* quality tires. (impersonal)

*We* stand behind *our* products and know *you* appreciate *our* quality tires. (personal)

### Use a Natural Tone

In Chapter Five I mentioned that your writing should *sound* like you. Using a "natural" tone means avoiding language that sounds awkward, old-fashioned, or contrived. After you've straightened out your grammar and polished up your sentences, your tone should still sound close to the way you might *speak* to someone. Of course, good on-the-job writing can't *duplicate* our speech patterns because we don't always speak by using *completed* sentences. We frequently use a few words, short phrases, or sentence fragments to express ourselves orally. Reproducing our speech patterns without some sort of "cleaning up" process would result in gibberish sometimes. But straightening out our writing doesn't mean adopting language that very few people would ever use orally.

1. *Receipt of* your letter is acknowledged. (artificial)

*I've received* your letter. (natural)

2. *The said report* was sent to the president this morning. (artificial)

*The report* was sent to the president this morning. (natural)

3. *Please find enclosed herewith* the *requested signed* document. (artificial)

*Here's* the signed document you wanted. (natural)

The *signed document* you asked for *is enclosed.* (natural)

### Use an Informal Tone

Why is it that the old myth about "formal" writing refuses to die? People who would never dream of having anything less than the "state of the art" in automobiles, computers, or wristwatches still cling to outdated ideas about on-the-job writing.

The myth goes something like this: On-the-job writing requires *formal* prose and a *formal* tone because on-the-job writing is serious business. It's all right to speak informally, but written communication should always be formal. We should never use contractions (can't, won't, shouldn't, etc.); we should never end sentences with prepositions (with, of, from, etc.); and we should avoid using "I" or "we" as much as possible.

Yet, when we analyze the writing of our best on-the-job writers, we find that they frequently use contractions, often end sentences with prepositions, and use "I" and "we" as much as necessary. Their writing is no less "serious" than other on-the-job writing, but it's usually better because these writers understand how to use our language effectively. They certainly understand the concept of tone, and how difficult it is to write in the appropriate tone if we're always writing "formally."

Very, very few on-the-job writing situations require the use of formal language, just as few speaking situations require a formal speech. There are many people who use formal language either because they've been told to by someone or because they think they're expected to use it (the myth again). But the writing *situation* rarely requires it.

Here are some examples of formal and informal writing. Notice how the tone changes:

1. *The General Midwest Insurance Company Group cannot* honor *the policyholder's* request for an extension of the date of repayment of the loan due to *the policyholder's* failure to remit January's loan payment. (formal)

Since this letter was sent to the policyholder, the writer could have used a more informal tone to get the message across.

*We can't* extend *your* loan repayment date because *you haven't* sent January's payment. (informal)

2. Our new crew supervisor *is not* a pleasant person for whom to work. (formal)

Our new crew supervisor *isn't* pleasant to work for. (informal)

3. This intricate accounting method *has not* been an easy method *with* which to disagree, but *we will* solve the problem *with* which *we have* been bothered. (formal)

This intricate accounting method *hasn't* been an easy method to disagree *with*, but *we'll* solve the problem *we've* been bothered *with*. (informal)

This intricate accounting method *hasn't* been easy to disagree *with*, but *we'll* solve the problem that has been bothering us. (informal)

### Use a Tactful Tone

"Tactful" writing is a good communication habit. Many times we're tempted to tear someone's head off with a few tactless words. In an oral discussion such words might vanish after the heated air cools. But a written document can be read again and again—the words don't disappear. Even worse, tactless documents might be passed around to a wider audience than we had in mind. Worse yet, written documents usually go into the files and can pop up at very inconvenient times, especially if the "situation" has changed.

However, a lot of tactless writing isn't done deliberately; it happens accidentally. We're either writing in a hurry or not thinking about the effects our words will have on our readers. In any event a tactless tone can become more tactful by simply altering a few words.

1. It seems like *you didn't understand* our instructions. We *specifically told you* to grease the machinery once a month to prevent rust. (tactless)

*Our instructions were* to grease the machinery once a month to prevent rust. (more tactful)

2. Your request for overtime pay is *completely out of line* because the contract *makes it very clear* that you will not be paid overtime until after 40 hours. (tactless)

Your request for overtime pay *can't be granted* because the contract *says* overtime will be paid after 40 hours. (more tactful)

3. Where are those figures you're *supposed to send me*? *Get them* to me *at once. You know* I can't prepare the monthly report without them. (tactless)

*Please send* me the figures *immediately* so that I can prepare the monthly report. (more tactful)

### Use a Positive Tone

Closely related to tactful writing is "positive" writing. Positive writing involves avoiding "negative" words—words that tend to rub people the wrong way. Positive writing also requires us to look for the positive side of a writing situation, instead of immediately reacting negatively. The message content doesn't change, of course; only the tone changes.

1. We *regret* to tell you that your automobile repair work *will not* be completed until Wednesday. (negative)

We're *glad* to tell you that your automobile repair work *will* be completed Wednesday. (positive)

2. Your promotion will be *held up* until October 1. (negative)

Your promotion will be *effective* October 1. (positive)

3. *It is against* our policy to pay more than one claim at a time. (negative)

*It is* our policy to pay only one claim at a time. (positive)

4. We have received your letter about the *alleged* loss of your car. (negative)

We've received your letter *about* the loss of your car. (neutral)

5. You *failed to tell* me what you want me to do about the situation. (negative)

*Please tell* me what you want me to do about the situation. (positive)

As you've probably noticed throughout this chapter, I've encouraged you to adopt a tone that avoids excessive formality and negative elements. Formal and negative elements appear so often in on-the-job writing that it's unnecessary to "learn" how to use them—we seem to have little trouble producing either formal or negative tones. Recognizing their overuse or inappropriate use is more difficult.

The key point this chapter is stressing, however, is that you should *control* your tone, regardless of the tone you adopt. You might decide to write formally, informally, negatively, or positively, but you should choose an appropriate tone for the writing situation and select words and phrases that reflect the tone you want.

Adopting an appropriate tone can help you communicate more effectively with your reader.

*Exercises*
1. Rewrite these sentences in a "personal" tone.
   a. Southwestern Manufacturing Company needs confirmation of its equipment order by September 30.

   b. On each of the monthly statements our firm sends to its customers, it is indicated that payment must be made within thirty days.

   c. It is recommended that the report of the committee be approved.

2. Rewrite these sentences in a "natural" tone.
   a. We invite your attention to the bank statement enclosed.

   b. Herewith noted is receipt of your monthly payment.

   c. Your perusal of said document is hereby requested.

3. Rewrite these sentences in an "informal" tone.

    a. The employment information we have obtained about you is not sufficient for our company to make a decision at this time.

    b. Reference is made to your letter of April 18 in which you requested information about our company's annual meeting of stockholders.

    c. It is necessary to remind you of the past due balance on your account about which we wrote to you a month ago.

4. Rewrite these sentences in a more "tactful" tone.

    a. We have checked out what you told us, and as we suspected, you are wrong.

    b. It sounds as if you didn't follow the instructions in the operator's manual about oiling the machinery.

    c. If you ever tell me what sizes you want, I'll make up your order.

5. Rewrite these sentences in a more "positive" tone.

    a. If you don't reply immediately, we won't be able to ship your equipment.

    b. You will never have reason to regret working for our company.

    c. Don't be delinquent with your report next month.

*Answers to Exercises*

1.    a. We need confirmation of our equipment order by September 30. (Please confirm our equipment order by September 30.)

    b. On each monthly statement we send to you, we'll indicate that payment is due within thirty days.

    c. I (We) recommend that you approve the committee's report.

2.  a. Please look at the enclosed bank statement.

    b. I've (We've) received your monthly payment.

    c. Please read this document.

3.  a. Your employment information isn't sufficient for us to make a decision now.

    b. In your April 18 letter you asked about our annual stockholder's meeting.

    c. As we informed you last month, your account payment is overdue.

4.  a. We've reviewed your information and discovered that you're incorrect.

    b. Did you follow the instructions in the operator's manual?

    c. Please tell me the sizes you want so that I can make up your order.

5.  a. Please reply immediately so that we can ship your order. (If you reply immediately, we can ship your order.)

    b. You'll be glad that you came to work for our company.

    c. Please be on time with your report next month.

# CHAPTER EIGHT

# Use Effective Paragraphs

Paragraphs are the building blocks of effective writing. Individual sentences, unless combined with other sentences, remain isolated and are incapable of fully expanding our routine ideas or adequately explaining our complex ones. Effective paragraphing can help us organize our ideas and keep them moving along in a logical way.

Good paragraphing makes us think about main ideas and supporting ideas. If we set up our paragraphs correctly, our readers will be able to understand our ideas more readily because they can see how one idea leads to the next one. The main idea, called the *topic sentence*, sets the stage for the content of the paragraph; the supporting ideas take their lead from the topic sentence and develop the paragraph.

The topic sentence is the key ingredient of the paragraph because it serves as a "road map" for the supporting ideas. Everything should be keyed to this sentence. If other sentences don't relate to the topic sentence, they should be thrown out. Otherwise, they will harm the *unity* of your paragraph. A *unified* paragraph is one that has a topic sentence *supported* and *developed* by other sentences that *directly relate* to the topic sentence.

Since it acts as a road map, the topic sentence should be the *first* sentence in the paragraph. Placing the topic sentence at the beginning of the paragraph has at least three advantages. First, you can refer back to this sentence to make sure you're sticking to the topic as you write your supporting sentences. Second, if your readers skim through your documents, they can pick up the main ideas quickly and go back for the details later. On the other hand, if your readers go through your documents thoroughly, the topic sentence gives them the "whole" idea and then the "parts" that make up that idea. Third, you can actually *organize* your entire document by writing all of your topic sentences *before* you fill in each paragraph's details.

This topic sentence organization method can be quite effective because it allows you to see the overall layout of your document before you spend a lot of time writing the supporting details. If you discover a hole in your logic, it's less painful to throw out topic sentences than whole paragraphs (I'll discuss organizing your material in more detail in Chapters Nine, Ten, and Eleven).

A good topic sentence is one that expresses an idea that can be *developed* or *enlarged upon* by the supporting ideas. Therefore, if the topic sentence—the main idea for the paragraph—can't be developed with details that answer "why," "what," or "how," it's probably not a very good topic sentence.

Let's take a look at how paragraphs are put together. Here's a topic sentence for a short paragraph:

> For income tax purposes, it's important for you to understand how your reimbursed business expenses should be handled.

This topic sentence could be developed by answering "why" it's important to understand or "how" the expenses should be handled. Here's the entire paragraph. I've underlined the part of the topic sentence that the writer chose to develop.

> For income tax purposes, it's important for you to understand how your reimbursed business expenses should be handled. If you're reimbursed for business expenses, you aren't required to report either the reimbursement or the expenses on your tax return. However,

any payment that exceeds your expenses will be included in your gross income and must be reported on your tax return.

This paragraph is unified because the supporting ideas relate to the main idea and enlarge upon the main idea. The paragraph is developed by supporting details that respond to the commitment the writer made for the paragraph in the topic sentence: "*how* your reimbursed business expenses should be handled." Once the writer established the paragraph commitment in the topic sentence, the responses of the supporting sentences had to fulfill that commitment or the paragraph wouldn't be unified.

Here's another example. I've underlined the key parts of the topic sentence and the supporting sentences that unify this paragraph.

Business owners and managers face many problems that are closely related to the kinds of businesses they run. For example, if they extend credit to customers, they will become interested in the proper management of credits and collections. If they are retailers or wholesalers, they may have delivery problems. If they are manufacturers, they will be concerned about efficient production.

If you adhere to this *commitment/response* relationship between your topic sentences and supporting sentences, you should be able to write unified paragraphs consistently. And if you can write unified paragraphs, you can write anything from a short letter to a complex report to an entire book. The next step is to use transitional devices to connect the sentences within the paragraphs and to connect one paragraph to to the next paragraph.

*Transitional devices* are words and phrases that help the reader to see the logical relationship between sentences and between paragraphs. Transitions maintain sentence and paragraph unity by serving a dual function: (1) They *refer back* to what has just been written, and (2) they *indicate* that either an *additional comment* or a *change* (or *exception*) in ideas is coming up.

All of this is pretty heavy work for a device that's supposed to be subtle, almost unnoticed, to be effective. Transitions should never be heavy-handed or disturbingly obvious, but they are the "glue" that connects related ideas.

Here's a paragraph that uses transitions effectively. I've underlined the transitional words. Notice how the words appear at the *beginning* of each sentence.

> Previous attempts to identify the personal traits of successful business managers have experienced considerable difficulty. One major problem is that of definition, which depends upon the meaning assigned by individuals; and individuals have widely differing concepts of the same terms. Second, overlapping of terms makes it difficult to draw sharp distinctions between various traits. Third, people are not just the sum total of their personality traits. Finally, of considerable importance is the previous inadequacy of criteria that indicate success.

With the transitional words in this paragraph, it's relatively easy to follow the writer's train of thought and keep the "problems" straight. Without these simple transitions, the writer's ideas might not stand out so clearly.

Here's another paragraph about successful business characteristics. Notice how this writer uses *key words* as transitions. I've underlined these words.

> The five personal characteristics that contribute to a businessperson's success are drive, thinking ability, human relations ability, communications ability, and technical knowledge. Drive is comprised of responsibility, vigor, initiative, persistence, and health. Thinking ability is comprised of original thinking, creative thinking, critical thinking, and analytical thinking.

<u>Human relations ability</u> is comprised of ascendancy, emotional stability, sociability, cautiousness, personal relations, consideration, cooperation, and tactfulness. <u>Communications ability</u> is comprised of verbal comprehension, oral communications, and written communications. <u>Technical knowledge</u> is all-encompassing.

Repetition of key words is an effective way to unify a paragraph, but it can sometimes become too heavy-handed. Using transitional words such as *first, second, third,* works for about three to five examples; then these words get fairly worn out. It's better to use a variety of transitional words to move your ideas along.

These two paragraphs about evaluation forms show more transitional word variety. In addition, notice how the two paragraphs are connected.

Generally, your manager will complete an evaluation form on your performance on every project you are in charge of. In the branches, <u>however</u>, about five evaluations a year per supervisor will be the target. A form may <u>also</u> be completed when you are working on projects others are in charge of, <u>but</u> this is not required.

The <u>form</u> will <u>also</u> be used for continuous assignments. The frequency of completion will be left to your manager's discretion, <u>but</u> some type of review process will occur at least semiannually (spaced not to coincide with your annual performance review). <u>Finally</u>, the form will <u>also</u> be used for special project assignments at your manager's discretion.

The writer used *also, however, but, finally,* and repetition of the key word *form* to connect the ideas. In the first paragraph there are *three* different uses of the evaluation form; in the second paragraph there are *two* uses. The writer could have listed these as *first, second, third,* etc., or used some other numerical transitional words, but the word variety is effective. However, the word *also* is used too often.

Other transitional words such as *moreover, furthermore,* or *in addition* could have been substituted for *also.*

Here's a list of words that can function as transitional devices. As you can see, there's quite a variety, and this list is certainly not all-inclusive. But it's important to select the right word to indicate the transition you're making.

To indicate *addition:* moreover, furthermore, also, too, besides, in addition, and

To indicate *comparison:* similarly, likewise, in comparison

To indicate *contrast:* but, yet, however, still, nevertheless, on the other hand, in contrast, otherwise, conversely, notwithstanding, to the contrary

To indicate *example:* for example, for instance, specifically, namely, as an illustration, to illustrate

To indicate *explanation:* in fact, that is, simply stated, in other words

To indicate *place:* inside, outside, to the right, to the left, under, over, nearby, beyond, adjacent to, opposite to

To indicate *results:* therefore, as a result, thus, consequently, so, because of, accordingly, thereupon, hence

To indicate *summary* (or conclusion): in short, in closing, in retrospect, in brief, to conclude, to summarize, on the whole

To indicate *time* (or sequence): first, second, then, next, now, later, in turn, finally, meanwhile, at length, the next day, in the meantime, subsequently, afterward

Now let's put all of these ideas together. In the following paragraph, identify all the *key elements* of the topic sentences, the *details* that support the topic sentence, and the *transitional devices* that help to unify the paragraph.

You should take certain precautions before purchasing secondhand equipment and fixtures. First, remember that you're buying secondhand materials that are worth only a percentage of their original value. Therefore, find out the equipment's age and obtain prices of similar equipment from other dealers. Try to determine how much the equipment and fixtures have depreciated. You must also be sure the equipment is in working order, and determine whether it's obsolete. It may be difficult to obtain repair parts for old models in case of break-down. And, finally, find out if any money is still owed on any of the equipment or fixtures.

I've underlined the key elements in the topic sentence and supporting sentences, and double-underlined the transitional devices:

You should take certain precautions before purchasing secondhand equipment and fixtures. First, remember that you're buying secondhand materials that are worth only a percentage of their original value. Therefore, find out the equipment's age and obtain prices of similar equipment from other dealers. Try to determine how much the equipment and fixtures have depreciated. You must also be sure the equipment is in working order, and determine whether it's obsolete. It may be difficult to obtain repair parts for old models in case of break-down. And, finally, find out if any money is still owed on any of the equipment or fixtures.

If the paragraph is unified, we should be able to answer these questions:

1. What does the topic sentence *commit* the paragraph to discussing?

*What* precautions should be taken before purchasing secondhand equipment and fixtures and *why* they should be taken.

2. What details *respond* to (or *support* ) the paragraph's commitment?

<u>Remember</u> what secondhand materials are <u>worth</u>.
<u>Find out</u> the equipment's <u>age</u>.
<u>Obtain</u> <u>prices</u> for similar equipment.
<u>Determine</u> how much the materials have <u>depreciated</u>.
<u>Be sure</u> the equipment is in <u>working order</u>.
<u>Determine</u> whether the equipment is <u>obsolete</u>.
<u>Find out</u> if <u>money</u> is still <u>owed</u>.

So far, we've looked at two ways to support the topic sentence and develop the paragraph: (1) *listing* reasons, uses, or other details and (2) *defining* terms. Both of these methods are effective, but there are many other ways to support the topic sentence and develop the paragraph.

Here are a few of the most common methods used to develop paragraphs. I'll also have more to say about this subject in Chapter Eleven.

### *"Listing" Method*

We've already seen the "listing" method, but it's worth another example. This method can be used with almost any kind of *time or sequence* transitional words. It's very effective if you have several points to make.

> The basic fire insurance policy is nearly identical in every state. The standard fire policy contains (1) an insuring clause, (2) stipulations and conditions that govern both your basic insurance contract and the extensions and endorsements, and (3) an attachment that describes the property being insured.

### *"Definition" Method*

We often have to define terms that our readers may not be familiar with or fully understand. The "five personal characteristics for business success" paragraph used as an example in this chapter combined the "definition" and "listing" methods. Here's a different approach.

> Many insurance contracts use deductibles. The deductible may be a percentage of the loss or a specified dollar

amount. In some contracts the deductible may be a waiting period. In others, it's subtracted from the loss settlement that would otherwise be payable or from the value of the insured property. Each policy must be checked to determine what kind of deductible it has.

### *"Example" Method*

The "example" method is one of the most effective ways to develop your paragraphs. Using examples or illustrations can make your paragraphs come alive because you *show* your reader what you're talking about. This method can be combined with any other method and usually improves the paragraph. For example, the "definition" paragraph above would be easier to understand had the writer used some examples of what a "deductible" looked like.

1. One of the major mistakes in choosing an employee is to hire the person without a clear knowledge beforehand of exactly what you want the person to do. For example, you should answer such questions as these before hiring anyone: If you are running a retail store, will a salesperson also do stockkeeping or bookkeeping? In a restaurant will a waiter or waitress also perform some of the duties of a host or hostess? Will the sawyer in a sawmill also be required to pile lumber? Answers to these kinds of questions are necessary to prevent misunderstandings.

2. Any effort to isolate personality traits faces the primary problem of definition. For example, honesty has different meanings for different people. Some people receiving a dime too much at the grocery would return it, but the same people receiving a dime too much from a vending machine might keep it and suffer no feelings of dishonesty. In many instances the meaning of honesty depends on the individual definition. Until a standardized concept is applied to the definition of personality traits, the problem will remain.

### *"General to Specific" Method*

To use this method, start with your topic sentence (your most *general* statement) and then write sentences that become *more specific* with *each* sentence, instead of writing sentences that have approximately the same weight. The development of the paragraph draws the reader more deeply into the subject.

> Before undertaking any new business venture, you should *consider several things* about the state of the economy. What are the *general* business conditions? What are the business conditions *in the city* and *neighborhood* where you are planning to locate? What are the current conditions *in the line of business* you're planning?

### *"Comparison/Contrast" Method*

"Comparison/contrast" shows the similarities and/or differences between two or more things. It's an effective method to use, particularly if you're trying to consider alternative ideas or various features of some pieces of equipment, etc.

> Besides general business conditions, there are other factors—over which the owners have no control—affecting individual firms. Examples of these are the relocations of highways, sudden changes in style, the replacement of existing products by new products, and local labor conditions. Although these factors may cause some businesses to fail, they may represent opportunities for others. One local marketplace may decline in importance, but at the same time new shopping centers are developing. Sudden changes in style or the replacement of existing products may mean troubles to certain businesses but open doors for new ones. Adverse employment situations in some areas may be offset by favorable situations in others. Ingenuity in taking advantage of changing consumer desires and technological improvements will always be rewarded.

### *"Cause/Effect" Method*

This method is a valuable one because causes and effects can solidly unify a paragraph through the *logic* of their relationships. On the other hand, the method can be tricky to use if the logic is questionable. It's vital that the causes and effects *fit* together.

> The causes of small business failures are well documented. Poor management appears to be the most common cause. Lack of management experience, unbalanced management experience, and incompetent management far outstrip other business failure causes such as lack of technical ability, fraud, or disasters.

> Writing unified paragraphs is probably the most important element in making sure your ideas are understood, especially if your job requires lengthy or complex writing. But even short letters are subject to the same principles of good paragraph development. It's not the length that's important; it's the unity.

> This chapter has concentrated on the writing of single, unified paragraphs because if we can write one unified paragraph, we can duplicate the process over and over again. In Chapter Eleven we'll see how these individual paragraphs can be combined into an overall organizational sequence.

### *Exercises*

Supply *transitional words* between each sentence. There may be more than one appropriate word in each case, but you should try to establish some sort of *unity* between the sentences.

> 1. Mr. Flynn arrived at the supermarket before closing time. He wasn't able to shop because he had left his wallet at home.

> 2. Ms. Norris worked very hard as our accounting supervisor. She was promoted to manager. She's doing quite well.

3. Our tire company faced stiff competition this year. Three other companies moved into our city. We managed to make a profit.

4. Suppliers depend on customers meeting their financial obligations. Prompt payment of accounts by customers is important to the supplier. The amount of working capital the supplier must maintain largely depends on how promptly the customers pay their bills. Suppliers often offer cash discounts for early payment of accounts.

5. Rent insurance can cover loss of use of real property damaged by fire or other peril. If you rent a building and your lease calls for continued payments even if fire makes the building untenantable, you can obtain coverage for this loss. If the lease calls for canceled or reduced rental payments, the owner can cover the loss of income with a different kind of rent insurance policy.

## Answers to Exercises

1. Mr. Flynn arrived at the supermarket before closing time. *However,* (but) he wasn't able to shop because he had left his wallet at home.

2. Ms. Norris worked very hard as our accounting supervisor. *Consequently,* (therefore, as a result) she was promoted to manager. *And* (Furthermore, moreover) she's doing quite well.

3. Our tire company faced still competition this year. *In fact,* three other companies moved into our city. *Still,* (however, but) we managed to make a profit.

4. Suppliers depend on customers meeting their financial obligations. *Therefore,* prompt payment of accounts by customers is important to the supplier. *In fact,* (simply stated) the amount of working capital the supplier must maintain largely depends on how promptly the customers pay their bills. *As a result,*

(consequently, therefore, so) suppliers often offer cash discounts for early payment of accounts.

5. Rent insurance can cover loss of use of real property damaged by fire or other peril. *For example,* (for instance) if you rent a building and your lease calls for continued payments even if fire makes the building untenantable, you can obtain coverage for this loss. *On the other hand,* (however, but) if the lease calls for canceled or reduced rental payments, the owner can cover the loss of income with a different kind of rent insurance policy.

# CHAPTER NINE

# Develop an Overall Plan

If you have the time to prepare a detailed outline before you write, the outline will help you organize your material more effectively than any other method can. But my experience indicates that most of us either don't have the time or won't take the time to prepare a thorough outline for most on-the-job writing tasks. Good organization of letters and memos is often neglected because we write them frequently and must produce them quickly.

Poorly organized writing has long been recognized as a significant interference problem that can confuse readers and make writing appear "illogical" or "not well thought out."

In this chapter and the two chapters that follow, I'll present a method that can help you organize your writing and save you time. At first, this method might not seem like a great time saver, but I think once you see how the pieces fit together, you'll realize how quickly you can organize your material by simply following the steps.

Developing an overall plan involves making decisions about *what* you're going to write *before* you write anything. It's a simple process (just a few short notes to yourself) that you can use on any written document, regardless of the document's length. Once you've become proficient in this method, you can organize your *entire* document much more quickly, and you can avoid the anxiety of not knowing what to say next.

Five steps make up this method. They should be performed in sequence.

1. Determine your purpose for writing.
2. Choose an overall approach.
3. Decide what information your "opening" should contain.
4. Decide what information your "closing" should contain.
5. Select an organizational sequence for your "body."

### Determine Your Purpose for Writing

Every on-the-job document you write should have a well-defined *primary* purpose. Sometimes a document will have a secondary purpose or perhaps be multipurposed, but you should be able to spell out *exactly* what the *primary* purpose of your document is. If you can't, then you're not ready to write. Trying to find your purpose *as you write* is a waste of time and often results in confusing, poorly organized documents.

You should be able to answer this question specifically: *Why* am I writing this letter/memo/report/etc.?

Here are a few unsatisfactory answers to this question:

Because my boss asked me to write.
Because John Simpson needs some information.
Because it's important to keep people informed.
Because I want to get my point across.
Because something needs to be done.

All of these responses are too vague; they could fit almost any on-the-job writing situation. Here's a better answer that shows the writer has a well-defined *primary* purpose:

I'm writing to give John Simpson information about our new monthly reporting system so that he can submit his reports correctly.

This statement clearly defines *why* the document is being written, *what information* the document should contain, and *what effects* (or results) are expected.

Take a look at this memo. Can you determine the writer's purpose? Does the writer accomplish that purpose?

TO:      S. Langstrom, W. Matlock, T. Robertson
FROM:   H. Williamson
SUBJECT: Meeting

Laura Barnes asked me to set up a meeting. I know it's difficult for all of us to get together because of our different schedules, but we need to have the meeting as soon as possible.

Laura won't be in next week, so we'll have to wait until at least the week after that, unless all of you can make it later this week.

Let me know when you will be available so that we can get together. I'll double-check with Laura about her schedule.

If Williamson is trying to set up a meeting, then this memo doesn't accomplish its purpose. If Williamson simply wants some available dates and times from Langstrom, Matlock, and Robertson, then the memo's still confusing because the writer leaves everyone up in the air about Laura Barnes's schedule, and she's the one who wants the meeting set up.

On the other hand, we can see the writer's purpose clearly in this letter:

Dear Mrs. Cohen:

You recently had your car serviced by Lars Gunderson, our transmission specialist.

We're proud of our reputation for high-quality repair work, and we constantly strive to improve our service. You can help us keep our standards high by letting us know how we could have improved our service to you.

Please take a moment to fill out the enclosed

questionnaire. For your convenience, we've also enclosed a postpaid, self-addressed envelope.

Thank you for your help.

Jeff Lewis
Service Manager

Lewis's primary purpose is to persuade Mrs. Cohen to fill out the service questionnaire and return it. His letter *reminds* Mrs. Cohen about her recent service, *stresses* the importance of her opinion, and specifically *requests* her help.

Although we have to look at the entire letter to understand Lewis's purpose for writing, Lewis determined his purpose by simply performing step one of his overall plan:

Question: Why am I writing this letter?
Answer: I'm writing to persuade Mrs. Cohen to fill out and return our service questionnaire.

The most effective on-the-job letter, memo, or report usually has only one main purpose, regardless of the complexity of the content. You should concentrate on determining your purpose and carrying it out. However, if your document has a *secondary* purpose, that purpose must be directly related to the primary purpose, or your document won't be unified.

The question/answer process can still be used:

Question: Why am I writing this letter?
Answer: (*Primary purpose*) To persuade Mrs. Cohen to fill out and return our service questionnaire.
(*Secondary purpose*) To create customer goodwill by showing Mrs. Cohen that we genuinely care about our customers.

Of course, you can extend this technique to multipurpose writing, too. But multipurpose letters, memos, and reports can become confusing very quickly. Even though many on-the-job writers try to cram a lot of questionably related material into one document, few can accomplish this difficult task well. Most on-the-job writing situations don't require multipurpose writing. I encourage you to stick·to determining your primary purpose and accomplishing that purpose.

### *Choose an Overall Approach*

Once you've determined your purpose for writing, you can proceed to step two. Choosing an overall approach involves deciding whether to reveal your decision, suggestion, recommendation, request for action, etc., *before* you've explained the situation or *after* you've explained the situation. In other words, do you tell your reader the bottom line immediately, or do you wait until you've given your reader information about the subject?

This step may sound sort of confusing, but it's actually quite simple because there are only two overall approaches to on-the-job writing: the *indirect* approach and the *direct* approach.

These two approaches are organized as follows:

*Indirect Approach*
    1. Introduce the subject of your letter, memo, or report.
    2. Explain or analyze your subject.
    3. Ask for action, tell the decision, make a recommendation, etc.

*Direct Approach*
    1. Ask for action, tell the decision, make a recommendation, etc., as you introduce the subject of your letter, memo, or report.
    2. Explain or analyze your subject.
    3. Close by elaborating on the action, decision, recommendation, etc., or use a goodwill message.

Here's the same letter written by using the *indirect* approach and the *direct* approach:

*Indirect Approach:*

    Dear Mr. Jablonski:

        We've carefully examined the suit you returned.

        The materials used in this suit are the finest, and the stitching appears to be of very high quality. We just don't know what caused the material to unravel the way it did. It's an extremely rare occurrence.

        We're sorry your suit proved to be unsatisfactory. However, we always stand behind our garments. Therefore, you may exchange your suit for another one or receive a total refund. Please bring this letter and your sales receipt to our store when you decide to either choose a new suit or request a refund.

    Nita Ferguson

    Store Manager

*Direct Approach*

    Dear Mr. Jablonski:

        We're sorry your suit proved to be unsatisfactory. However, we always stand behind our garments. Therefore, you may exchange your suit for another one or receive a total refund.

        The materials used in this suit are the finest, and the stitching appears to be of very high quality. We just don't know what caused the material to unravel the way it did. It's an extremely rare occurrence.

        Please bring this letter and your sales receipt to our store when you decide to either choose a new suit or request a refund.

    Nita Ferguson

    Store Manager

If you were Mr. Jablonski, which letter would you like to receive? Most people prefer the second letter (direct approach) because it *immediately* tells Mr. Jablonski that the store will take care of his problem. He may or may not pay much attention to the explanation (which is the same in both versions) because his problem has been solved. Using the *direct* approach can be quite effective when you have "good news" for your reader because most of us like to receive good news that has favorable results.

In fact, the first letter (indirect approach) sounds like Mr. Jablonski is being set up for "bad news." It doesn't turn out that way, but since Nita Ferguson already *knows* what the bottom line will be in this letter, she should choose the more effective overall approach.

To develop her overall plan before writing her letter, Ms. Ferguson might have used steps one and two this way:

1. Question: Why am I writing this letter?
   Answer: (*Primary purpose*) To solve Mr. Jablonski's problem with his suit by offering him an exchange or refund.

   (*Secondary purpose*) To maintain our store's reputation by emphasizing that faulty merchandise is unusual and that we stand behind our merchandise.

2. Question: Which overall approach should I use?
   Answer: (*Direct approach*) Because I can solve Mr. Jablonski's problem (good news), and he's probably more interested in *how* I'm going to take care of his problem.

On the other hand, what if Ms. Ferguson had decided to deny Mr. Jablonski's claim and leave him stuck with his shredded suit? Obviously, Mr. Jablonski would consider this "bad news" and wouldn't be eager to receive it. In this writing situation Ms. Ferguson would want to make sure that Mr. Jablonski at least *reads* her explanation before he reads the bad news. If her first sentence turns him off ("I'm sorry but we can't make an exchange or refund"), he may not read the explanation. At any rate, once he knows the bottom line, he's no longer a *neutral* reader. In this instance Ms. Ferguson should use the indirect approach (*introduce* the subject, *explain* the circumstances, *tell* the decision).

For "bad news," controversial material, complex explanations, or unfamiliar material, the indirect approach is often more effective because most people are conditioned to read from "top to bottom." We usually read (not always, of course) by starting at the beginning and then following the writer's lead until we get to the end of the material.

As an on-the-job writer, you can take advantage of these reading habits to present your case *before* your reader sees your conclusion. Your chances of convincing or persuading your reader are far greater if you can *involve* the reader in the *logic* of your ideas and presentation. Even if your reader ends up disagreeing with your conclusion, recommendation, or whatever, at least you've had the opportunity to *explain* the situation as you see it.

It's no accident that nearly 80 percent of on-the-job reports are written using the indirect approach. Using this approach allows you to set the stage for your reader by providing valuable background information before plunging into the heart of your discussion or analysis.

Just as many on-the-job writers never (or rarely) clearly determine their purposes for writing, many writers also never think about their overall approaches and the effects their approaches can have on their readers' receptiveness to their messages. Instead, they plunge in, start writing, and hope everything will work out by the time they finish their messages.

Take a look at this memo recommending the cancellation of a long-standing account. Notice how effectively the writer uses the indirect approach.

TO:        H. L. Krantz
FROM:      W. V. Henderson
SUBJECT:  Carrigan Account

I've recently completed a detailed analysis of the Carrigan account's revenues and expenditures over the past fifteen years. The figures are enclosed. [*Introduces* the subject; *provides* background information.]

In the last five years this account has produced almost no revenue, and managing the account has actually cost us money. In addition, although I realize that Mr. Carrigan has been our client for many years, his account has never been a large one. And, as the figures show, the account has steadily dwindled. [*Summarizes* the analysis; *explains* the situation.]

Frankly, I don't think the account will ever recover. I recommend that we exercise our option to withdraw from the account. [*Draws* a conclusion; *makes* a recommendation.]

Before writing this memo, Henderson might have used steps one and two this way:

1. Question: Why am I writing this memo?
   Answer: (*Primary purpose*) To persuade Krantz that we should withdraw from the Carrigan account because it's unprofitable.

2. Question: Which overall approach should I use?
   Answer: (*Indirect approach*) Because Krantz must be persuaded, it's important to present my case logically by providing background information and explaining the situation so that my conclusion and recommendation make sense.

Here are the major uses of the indirect and direct approaches to on-the-job writing:

*Indirect Approach*
Use the indirect approach when you want to involve your reader in the logic of your ideas so that your reader understands your "reasoning" *before* you present your decision, conclusion, recommendation, etc. This approach is effective with the following messages:
   "Bad news" messages
   Persuasive messages
   Controversial messages

Complex explanations
Unfamiliar material (usually, a lot of explanation will be necessary)

*Direct Approach*
Use the direct approach when you want to let your reader know the bottom line *immediately.* This approach is effective with these messages:
"Good news" messages
Noncontroversial messages
Summary material
Familiar material (not much, if any, explanation should be necessary)

Although I've taken a chapter to explain how to use steps one and two of the overall plan, the actual process can be performed very quickly because you're simply making decisions *before* you write. Until you become familiar with the overall method, I suggest that you write out answers to the questions you ask yourself to determine your purpose and choose an overall approach. But for some messages (particularly short ones) these first two steps serve more as a mental checklist you go through before proceeding to steps three, four, and five.

So far, developing your overall plan has involved asking and answering two questions in sequence:

1. Why am I writing this letter/memo/report/etc.? (*Determine* your *purpose.*)
2. Which overall approach should I use (*indirect* or *direct*)?

After a couple exercises, we can move on to the next chapter for steps three and four: deciding what information your opening and closing should contain.

*Exercises*
1.   a. What is (are) the *purpose(s)* of this letter?
     b. Which *overall approach* is used?

Dear Mr. Lang:

We're sorry about the experience you had with your Writewell 900 typewriter.

The Writewell is guaranteed against manufacturing defects for one year after purchase. Although your typewriter's carriage return was damaged during the warranty period, the damage wasn't caused by defective materials. As you mentioned in your letter, your daughter dropped the machine on the sidewalk.

Our warranty doesn't cover accidental damage beyond our control. We can, however, repair the carriage return if it isn't damaged too badly. We would charge for this repair work, of course, but the charges may be substantially less than the value of your machine.

I'll be glad to give you an estimate if you would like to bring your typewriter to our office.

Phillip Hughes
Service Manager

**2.** The following sentences are *first sentences* in their respective letters, memos, and reports. Can you determine which *overall approach* is being used?

a. We are in the process of reviewing your report.

b. Our report about the employee morale problem is enclosed.

c. Our studies indicate that your operation isn't profitable.

d. We recommend that the bottling plant be closed permanently.

e. You should buy those stocks we talked about last week.

f. Your recommendations have been accepted without change.

g. Our report about the parking lot problem contains inaccurate information.

h. We've received your letter about your experience with our product.

i. We've reviewed Mrs. Smith's personnel file very carefully.

j. We know you have been disappointed in our service, but let us explain what happened.

*Answers to Exercises*

1. a. (*Primary purpose*) To explain to Mr. Lang that the damage to his typewriter isn't covered under our warranty.

   (*Secondary purpose*) To help Mr. Lang get his typewriter repaired by offering our services.

   b. (*Indirect approach*) Because Mr. Lang probably wants his typewriter repaired under the provisions of the warranty, I want him to understand what the warranty covers *before* he is denied coverage. Moreover, my alternative solution won't make any sense until Mr. Lang understands why the warranty doesn't apply.

2. a. Indirect (no decision, conclusion, recommendation, etc.)
   b. Indirect (no decision, conclusion, recommendation, etc.)
   c. Direct (conclusion)
   d. Direct (recommendation)
   e. Direct (recommendation)
   f. Direct (decision)
   g. Direct (conclusion)
   h. Indirect (no decision, conclusion, recommendation, etc.)
   i. Indirect (no decision, conclusion, recommendation, etc.)
   j. Indirect (no decision, conclusion, recommendation, etc.)

# CHAPTER TEN

# Use Effective Openings and Closings

Understanding how to use effective openings and closings is vital to organizing your letters, memos, and reports. Your openings and closings depend on the decisions you've made about your overall plan. Once you've determined your purpose and chosen an overall approach, you've committed yourself to using certain openings and closings to develop your plan effectively. It's just a matter of making choices.

For example, if you've selected the *indirect approach* for your letter, memo, or report, any opening information that draws a conclusion or makes a recommendation isn't appropriate. Or if you've chosen the *direct approach*, then using extensive background material in your opening won't fit your overall approach because background information doesn't qualify as a "bottom line" opening.

Thus, the decisions you made in steps one and two of your overall plan will now help you make decisions for steps three and four. These steps require you to decide what *type of information* your opening and closing should contain. Again, you're making *decisions* about the *organization* of your letter, memo, or report; you're not actually writing at this point. And although we're going to proceed through these steps in "slow motion," you can perform the process very rapidly once you've become familiar with it.

First, some definitions are in order. An *opening* can be one sentence, several sentences, one paragraph, or several paragraphs, depending on the length and complexity of your material. The same holds true for a *closing*. To qualify as an opening or closing, the information must be the *type* that *belongs* at the beginning or end of a letter, memo, or report.

For instance, a detailed *analysis* (or *explanation*) doesn't qualify as an opening or closing because it neither *introduces* nor *concludes* the subject. Analyses and explanations belong to the "body" portion of your document (I'll discuss how to organize the body in the next chapter). Similarly, statistical data, tables, graphs, etc., are usually *supporting* material; they don't make effective openings and closings.

In this chapter I'll be talking about selecting the *type* of information that goes into your opening or closing, not the full *content* of the message. To illustrate my points, I'll have to use complete sentences and paragraphs with lots of details, but you should remember that your *decisions* about steps three and four involve selecting *types* of information that will help your opening and closing fit into your overall plan.

Let's start with openings. Although there are many types of information that qualify as openings, I'll stick to the most common and most effective openings used with the indirect and direct approaches to on-the-job writing.

## INDIRECT APPROACH OPENINGS........................

### Introduce the Subject

This opening may not be the most exciting, but it's probably the best opening you can use. It lets your reader know immediately what the subject matter is. Actually, *all* of the indirect *and* direct openings used as examples in this chapter *introduce the subject,* but some of them provide other information at the same time. However, in the *indirect* approach, notice that introducing the subject doesn't *commit* the writer to anything *except* the subject. We still don't know which direction the letter, memo, or report will take.

1. We've received your letter about *your damaged furniture.*

2. Our report about the *third quarter budget* is enclosed.

3. We've reviewed *last year's administrative procedures.*

4. I've analyzed *several aspects* of the *Lexington Bridge contract* that you may be interested in.

5. The *Tonapan land survey project* has produced *some results* I'd like to bring you up-to-date on.

### Provide a Reminder

Sometimes we can introduce the subject by jogging someone's memory. This can be an effective way to get someone's attention, while at the same time opening the discussion.

1. *As you know,* we've been involved in a *financial contingency study* since last July.

2. *If you recall,* John Harrison mentioned he would be *monitoring* our *accident reporting system.*

3. Last year *we agreed* not to let another year pass without *clarifying* our *contract with Bailey Construction.*

### Mention the Authorization

Still another way to introduce the subject is to mention how a project or report got authorized in the first place. Often, such authorization openings can enhance the credibility of your document and give it added importance. Most formal reports, for example, are usually authorized or requested because of the amount of work involved in putting these reports together. Presenting your boss with a fifty-page unauthorized, unrequested report isn't a good way to start your day.

1. As the *board of directors requested* last March, we have examined *each department's cost effectivensss.* Our report is enclosed.

2. A few weeks ago *you asked me* to look into *methods to improve our department's productivity.*

3. Last year's *planning committee authorized* a *study* to determine the *effectiveness* of our *planning process.*

### Provide Background Information

Providing background information for our readers is often necessary to set the stage for our analysis or explanation. This information should bring the reader up-to-date so that the reader can follow the discussion more easily. Of course, how much information you provide depends on your reader's prior knowledge of the subject or situation. But if background material is needed, you should put it in your opening.

1. *Last winter* we *began* a *study to determine the savings* that might result from *turning down the thermostat to 50 degrees after working hours.*

2. *During* the *past three months,* the *personnel department* has been *evaluating a corporate-wide training program.*

3. Since our *present telephone system* requires *all calls* to be *handled manually, we've asked* the *telephone company to recommend* a more *efficient call-handling procedure.*

An indirect opening paragraph *combining* a few of these elements would look like this:

As C. V. Travis requested, we examined the sewage drainage system thoroughly this year to determine whether any sewage was seeping into the local water supply. You may recall that the three of us discussed this possible seepage problem last February, and you mentioned your interest in seeing any information we could come up with. I've enclosed a copy of our report.

*Subject:* sewage drainage system report
*Authorization:* "As C. V. Travis requested..."
*Background:* " ... examined ... system ... determine whether any sewage was seeping into the local water supply."
*Reminder:* "You may recall ... discussed ... last February ... your interest in seeing ... information...."

## DIRECT APPROACH OPENINGS ........................

Direct approach openings introduce the subject, too, but they also provide "bottom line" information that would be inappropriate for indirect openings. If you select the direct approach as your overall approach, use one or more of these openings.

### Tell the Decision

1. We've *decided to go ahead* with *your work/study project.*
2. We're sorry, but *your insurance policy can't be renewed.*
3. The financial planning committee *has agreed* to *put your capital expenditures request in* next year's budget.

### Tell/Request Action

1. *Enclosed* is *your refund check* for $50.75.
2. *Your automobile policy* has been *amended,* as you requested.
3. To reduce our electricity bill, we *turned off* the *plant lights at 10 P.M.* every night last week.
4. Please *send* us *your November loan payment* within ten days.

5. Please *fill out* the enclosed *personal history questionnaire* and *return* it to our office.

## Draw Conclusions

1. Our *computer operations* department *hasn't been able to solve* the *production scheduling problem.*
2. Our *studies indicate* that we *need additional information about* the *water treatment plant* before we can make any recommendations.
3. After examining Mr. Dorn's personnel file carefully, we can find no discrepancies in his employment dates; therefore, we've *concluded* that the *security charges are groundless.*

## Make Recommendations

1. After careful study of our photocopying needs, we *recommend* that you *purchase* the *Infoset photocopier.*
2. We *recommend* that the *bottling plant* be *closed permanently.*
3. To increase our efficiency in handling reports, we *should move* the *data control* section *closer to* the *computer operations* department.

A direct opening paragraph *combining* some of these elements would look like this:

After analyzing the data from the proposed Sunset Dam, we've concluded that the project will be too much of a financial drain on our resources for another five years. Therefore, we recommend that the proposed project be terminated, effective immediately.

*Subject:* proposed Sunset Dam project
*Conclusion:* " ... concluded ... too much ... financial drain ... for ... five years."
*Recommendation:* " ... recommend ... terminated, effective immediately."

Now let's combine step one (*determine* your purpose for

writing), step two (*choose* an overall approach), and step three (*decide* what information your opening should contain).

TO:       Bill Davis
FROM:     Mary Clifton
SUBJECT: Work Environment Quality

In the past two years our company has grown more rapidly than we had anticipated. Last March, Terry Jones authorized a study to determine whether our rapid growth had caused any serious deterioration in the quality of our work environment. If you recall, several months ago you also expressed an interest in this subject.

We've recently completed our study, and I'm enclosing a copy for your use. I'd be very interested in your evaluation of our findings, especially if you could comment before next month's staff meeting. Just a short memo would be fine.

1. Question: Why am I writing this memo?
Answer: (*Primary purpose*) To ask Bill Davis to comment on our work environment study.

2. Question: Which overall approach should I use?
Answer: (*Indirect approach*) Because Bill needs to have some background information about the study before I ask him to comment on it.

3. Question: What information should my opening contain?
Answer: (*Subject*) Work environment study.
(*Authorization*) Terry Jones authorized the study.
(*Background*) The study began last March to determine whether our rapid growth had deteriorated work environment quality.
(*Reminder*) Bill was interested several months ago.

Step four involves deciding what information to use in your closing. Here are the most common closings used with the indirect and direct approaches to on-the-job writing.

### INDIRECT APPROACH CLOSINGS.......................

Since the indirect openings introduced the subject, provided background information, etc., the indirect closings now have to contain the "bottom line" information. Indirect closings are almost identical to direct openings. The major difference is that the closing comes after your "body," so that you can often *refer* to the information you've already presented. It's important, however, to close *emphatically;* your reader shouldn't wonder what the bottom line is.

### Tell the Decision

1. Your bill *won't become due until* after *you've re-ceived* your *order.*
2. We'll *keep* your *application on file until* we *hear from you.*
3. We've *decided* to *delay the move until* the *economic climate improves.*

### Ask for Action

1. By September 1, please *let me know what you find out* about the missing inventory records.
2. Please *send me your check* for $45.85 to cover the freight charges.
3. *Send me* your *hospital report* by December 15.

### Draw Conclusions

1. From the results so far, *two conclusions are possible:* (1) Our employee benefit plan is competitive, and (2) employees have no preferences among the benefit plans offered.
2. The $4,568 savings *should help us reach our goal* three months early.

3. We *don't believe* there is a relationship between the lighting level and the productivity of our office personnel.

### Make Recommendations

1. We *recommend you adopt* the new payment schedule outlined in our report.
2. We *should purchase* the Lennox 850 photocopy machine by August 19.
3. The accounting department *should be relocated* to the southwest corner of Building 308.

### Tell the Action

1. To solve this insulation problem, we've *installed* a *new Tractway door.*
2. I've *purchased one hundred uniforms* with full insignia to replace our old uniforms.
3. Our banquet committee *has reserved Old Hickory restaurant* for our annual party.

Here's an indirect approach closing paragraph that contains some of these elements:

As you can see from this analysis, the Harlinson agricultural project looks very profitable. I recommend we purchase 15,000 acres of bottomland near Fulton Bend. Since we need to move quickly, I need your decision by May 15.

*Subject:* Harlinson agricultural project
*Conclusion:* " ... project looks very profitable."
*Recommendation:* "I recommend ... purchase 15,000 acres ... near Fulton Bend."
*Request for Action:* " ... your decision by May 15."

## DIRECT APPROACH CLOSINGS .........................

In the direct approach opening the bottom line is revealed immediately. Therefore, simply repeating this opening information in the closing isn't very effective. Since the "heavy guns" have already been used in the direct opening, and then the analysis or explanation in the "body" has provided most of the supporting information, the direct closing is often weak ("If you have any further questions, please let me know," etc.). But the direct closing can be effective if you stay with the writing situation to the end and avoid using the so-called throwaway endings (closings that could be attached to *any* letter, memo, report).

### Elaborate on the Action/Decision/Conclusion/ Recommendation

The most effective direct approach closing is to stay with your letter, memo, or report all the way to the end. For example, if you tell someone in your direct approach opening that you're going to take care of the problem, wait until your closing to tell the person *when* or *how* you're going to take care of it. If you reveal everything in your opening, you'll end up with nothing left to say in your closing except the routine, worn-out throwaway sentences that we see so often ("Thanking you in advance for your attention to this matter," etc.).

1. I'll *make sure* that your replacement *battery is shipped* by October 25.

2. *At* our *next meeting* the full committee *will review your recommendations*, of course, but the preliminary figures look fine.

3. Your report is certainly important, and I'll *send it to Phil Duncan* as soon as I've studied it more.

### Make Further Correspondence Unnecessary

Instead of weakly ending your letter, memo, or report with a routine closing, why not firm up your closing by eliminating confusion about the next step. If the situation can be taken care of with one piece of correspondence, then you should make further correspondence (or contact) unnecessary.

1. I'll *see you* Friday at noon *unless you call me.*

2. We'll *move ahead* with the implementation of the new budget *as agreed unless we hear from you* by January 15.

3. *Let me know* by tomorrow *if you can't attend* the planning meeting.

Of course, you have to use this closing appropriately. There must be some sort of *understanding* between you and your reader about the situation.

### Use a Goodwill Message

Yes, goodwill messages are appropriate closings for the direct approach and are probably next in popularity to the throwaway closing. Sometimes a goodwill close just "sounds" right or looks like the most effective way to end our comments. However, goodwill closes are overused, abused, and frequently misused. If the element of sincerity is missing, the goodwill close is inappropriate. If the goodwill closing is too "mushy" or "gushy," it's not appropriate for on-the-job writing. And if this closing is too wordy, it's ineffective. The best goodwill closings are short and to the point. They are usually more effective when *combined* with another closing.

1. *Thank you* for your help.
2. *We enjoyed* talking with you last week.
3. Let me know *if I can help you*.
4. *I'm looking forward* to seeing you (meeting you, hearing from you, etc.).
5. *Thank you* for taking care of this matter so promptly.

Here's a *direct approach* closing paragraph combining these elements:

Thanks for all of your help last week. We've already started purchasing the necessary laboratory equipment. Unless we hear from you, we'll put the new laboratory procedures into effect on November 1.

*Subject:* new laboratory procedures
*Goodwill Message:* "Thanks for ... your help...."
*Elaborate on Action/Decision:* "We've ... started purchasing...."

*Further Correspondence Unnecessary:* "Unless we hear from you ... we'll put ... into effect...."

Here are four steps of the overall plan applied to a recommendation memo:

1. Determine your purpose for writing.
2. Choose an overall approach.
3. Decide what information your opening should contain.
4. Decide what information your closing should contain.

TO:   Helen McDonnell
FROM:  William Rothman
SUBJECT: Microfilm Retrieval System

We can achieve more efficient handling of our historical inventory records through use of an electronically indexed, automated microfilm retrieval system. This system could save us as much as $100,000 a year and simplify our complex record-keeping procedures. I recommend we appoint a special project group to study such a system this year.

  This system can hold several hundred thousand records dating back to our very first order. It can bring all of our records together in one place and take up only a fraction of the storage space we now use. Best of all, we can easily create a duplicate backup system for security.

  I'm enclosing some preliminary cost estimates, but we need the project group to study all the details and make sure we get a system compatible with our operation.

Now let's analyze this memo using the four steps we've covered so far:

1. Question: Why am I writing this memo?

Answer: (*Primary purpose*) To persuade Helen McDonnell to appoint a project group to study a microfilm retrieval system.

2. Question: Which overall approach should I use?

Answer: (*Direct approach*) Because the cost savings will be significant ($100,000) and our present system is too complex, Helen will probably be receptive to this "good news."

3. Question: What information should my opening contain?

Answer: (*Subject*) Appointing a microfilm retrieval system study group. (*Conclusion*) We can save $100,000 and simplify our inventory record procedures with this new system. (*Recommendation*) Appoint a study group.

4. Question: What information should my closing contain?

Answer: (*Elaborate on recommendation*) Enclose cost estimates. Stress need for study group.

In this memo Rothman could have also used the indirect approach very effectively. In fact, most *persuasive* messages usually work out better with the indirect approach (see Chapter Nine). However, in this case, Rothman recognized that his reader (Helen McDonnell) would be receptive to the direct approach because the new system would offer substantial advantages ($100,000 savings, etc.) that he could summarize quickly and support easily. In other words, the bottom line is so obviously appealing that Helen McDonnell would want to read more.

Well, we've covered four of the five steps to develop your overall plan. After a few exercises, we can move on to the final step: selecting an organizational sequence for the body of your letter, memo, or report.

*Exercises*

1. Identify the *overall approach* and the *type of information* used in these openings.

    a. Last October, S. L. Winston requested us to develop a system capable of tracking our delinquent accounts. A few months prior to that, you had expressed an interest in looking at this kind of system for your operation. I'm enclosing the system manual for your use.

    b. It's apparent that our equipment testing area has become overcrowded and should be expanded. After careful study, we recommend annexing at least one thousand square feet from the Building 42 staging area.

2. Identify the *overall approach* and the *type of information* used in these closings.

    a. Your comments were very helpful. Unless you have some objection, I'll mention your suggestions about improving our documentation procedures to our full task group at the next meeting.

    b. As this analysis shows, our in-house personnel don't have the expertise to do the computer programming we need. Therefore, I've contracted with CGT Systems, Inc., to do the initial programming and to provide training for our people.

3.     a. What is the *purpose* of this memo?
    b. Which *overall approach* is used?
    c. What *type of information* does the opening contain?
    d. What *type of information* does the closing contain?

    TO:       Henry Lundergun
    FROM:   Charlotte Heath
    SUBJECT: Automobile Lease/Purchase Report

Last year we couldn't provide adequate cost justification for purchasing our automobile fleet. In fact, we ended up postponing the purchase for six months.

You may recall that Larry Hines authorized a study to determine whether it would be more cost efficient to lease or purchase our company cars. Larry's group completed the study a few days ago. I've enclosed a copy of the report.

The report makes a strong case for leasing instead of purchasing our next automobile fleet. After looking at all the numbers, I've come to the same conclusion. I've already contacted four car dealers for fleet leasing rates. I should have that information to you by next week.

## Answers to Exercises

1.  a. *Overall Approach:* Indirect
    *Subject:* Delinquent accounts' tracking system
    *Authorization:* "S. L. Winston requested us..."
    *Reminder:* " ... you had expressed an interest...."

    b. *Overall Approach:* Direct
    *Subject:* Equipment testing area expansion
    *Conclusion:* " ... has become overcrowded and should be expanded."
    *Recommendation:* " ... recommend annexing ... one thousand square feet ... Building 42...."

2.  a. *Overall Approach:* Direct
    *Subject:* Documentation procedures improvement
    *Goodwill:* "Your comments ... helpful."
    *Further correspondence unnecessary:* "Unless you ... objection...."
    *Elaborate on Action/Decision:* " ... I'll mention ... at the next meeting."

    b. *Overall Approach:* Indirect
    *Subject:* Computer programming needs

*Conclusion:* " ... in-house personnel don't have expertise to do ... programming we need."
*Tell the Action:* "I've contracted with CGT Systems...."

3.  a. *Primary Purpose:* To explain to Henry Lundergun why I've concluded that leasing our automobile fleet is more cost efficient than purchasing, and that I'm gathering information about specific costs.

    b. *Indirect Approach:* Because I need to give Henry some background information and make him aware of the Hines report so that my conclusion and action are supported.

    c. *Subject:* Automobile lease/purchase report results
    *Background:* "Last year we couldn't provide ... cost justification...." " ... postponing ... purchase for six months."
    *Reminder:* "You may recall...."
    *Authorization:* " ... Larry Hines authorized a study...."

    d. *Conclusion:* "The report makes a strong case for leasing...." " ... I've come ... same conclusion."
    *Tell the Action:* "I've ... contacted four car dealers...." "I should have ... information to you ... next week."

# CHAPTER ELEVEN

# Organize Your Material

The final step in developing your overall plans is to select an effective organizational sequence for the *body* of your material.

What is an "organizational sequence"? It's simply a method to organize the information you're going to use in the body of your letter, memo, or report. You can *select* the sequence *before* you write, thus saving yourself valuable time.

And what is the "body"? Most of your discussion, explanation, description, or analysis belongs in the body. In a sense, the body is the *foundation* of your document. Whereas your opening and closing take care of the action, decision, conclusion, or recommendation, the body provides the supporting material that makes your opening and closing successful.

After setting up your opening and closing, how do you come to grips with that mass of information, statistics, and so forth that must be discussed, explained, and analyzed? Although we often struggle with our writing, most on-the-job material can be organized quickly by using a few organizational sequences. Once we recognize that certain information lends itself to being organized the *same way* over and over again, we can make our task much easier.

For example, let's assume your boss sends you to an all-day budget planning meeting to find out how the plan will affect your department. After attending the meeting for the whole day, you come away with only six or seven items that may affect your department. When you write your report to your boss, how do you organize this material?

If you understand how to use organizational sequences, you will have already made this decision by the time you read this sentence.

Later, you may agonize over such *writing* chores as selecting the right words to express yourself clearly or making sure your sentences are grammatically sound. But the best way to *organize* the material you've gathered is to *rank* these six or seven items from the most important to the least important (*priority sequence*).

Why? How can I be so sure? There must be dozens of ways to organize this material. If we start writing *before* we select our sequence, we may end up going through most of the other ways (and spend a lot of time). But would we come up with a *better* way to organize this material? Maybe, but I don't think so.

After all, what are the choices? You could discuss the items in no particular order at all (randomly) or as they were presented at the meeting (chronologically). However, ranking the items by their importance to your department gives your boss the most important information first. If you *know* your boss would *prefer* to see the items discussed in some other way, then the sequence decision has already been made for you. Most of the time, though, we're not given this kind of specific direction.

Many on-the-job writing situations can be approached this way. Certain on-the-job material consistently fits into a prescribed organizational sequence. And certain organizational sequences can be used more often than others because most on-the-job material fits a pattern that occurs repeatedly. When we write, we sometimes complicate our task because we don't think about these patterns.

In Chapter Eight I discussed ways to develop and unify paragraphs. Organizational sequences are extensions of the same kind of development and unity principles that are important in effective paragraphs.

Here are seven of the most commonly used organizational sequences in on-the-job writing:

Chronological (Sequential) Sequence
Priority Sequence
Reverse Priority Sequence
Problem/Cause/Solution Sequence
Comparison/Contrast/Sequence
Advantages/Disadvantages Sequence
Negative/Positive Sequence

### Chronological (Sequential) Sequence

This sequence is one that most of us probably consider first when trying to organize our material because we're used to thinking about things *in the order* they occur (Step one, step two, etc.; July 21, August 3, September 9, etc.). It's an effective sequence when used to explain a *series* of events or actions involved in a situation.

Dear Mr. Johnson:

I've been experiencing a problem with your store that I think you should be aware of.

On September 3, I bought a digital watch for $59.95. I returned the watch on September 21 because it had stopped running. The clerk gave me another watch, and I filled out the paperwork necessary to straighten out the exchange. The replacement watch also cost $59.95. On October 1, I received my monthly charge statement and found out that your store had charged me for the original watch *and* the replacement watch. In addition, I was charged $79.95, instead of $59.95.

I promptly sent my check for $59.95 and included a letter explaining that the correct charge should have been $59.95, not $159.90 (two watches at $79.95).

My November 1 billing, however, still carried the incorrect charge. I sent another letter explaining the situation, and I even called your store manager, Silvia

Ponds. Ms. Ponds told me she would correct the mistake, but my December 1 bill still carried the charge. I called Ms. Ponds, but she wasn't there, and she never returned my call.

My January 1 bill just arrived today. The incorrect charge is on it. I feel that I've been patient, but I don't know what else I can do to get this situation taken care of.

Will you please look into this matter? My phone number is 459-0809.

Thank you,
Louise Rogers

### Priority Sequence

As I've already mentioned, this sequence works well when you want to *rank* items (reasons, recommendations, etc.) from the most important to the least important. It can also be used by establishing some sort of criterion and then *listing* your items based upon that criterion. In the memo below, Charles Horner establishes *volume* as his most important criterion and then simply *lists* his items according to volume.

TO:     William Ledbetter
FROM:   Charles Horner
SUBJECT: Appliance Department Sales Results

I'm sure you'll be interested in the results of our sales campaign in the appliance department. If you recall, we started this campaign three months ago with extensive advertising in the local papers.

Since our initial advertising on May 15, we've sold 432 microwave ovens, washer/dryer combinations, and refrigerators.

Microwave ovens led in volume with 278 sold. They were our strongest seller evey month. In fact, we barely had enough stock to handle the demand. Crenshaw ovens accounted for 123 sales; Lorilee Model 500 totaled 101; and Sureheat trailed with 54.

Washer/dryer combinations totaled 124 sales. Supply and demand just about balanced every month. Interestingly, the Carrington Readywash made up 104 of the total sales. The other 20 units were spread out over six other brands.

Only 30 refrigerators were sold, even after all of that advertising. We have quite an oversupply right now. I'm not sure what to make of this poor performance.

I believe we suspected that microwave ovens would be our leader; now we know for sure. We should stock up heavily before our next campaign.

### Reverse Priority Sequence

In this sequence the items (reasons, recommendations, etc.) are ranked from *least* important to *most* important. Reverse priority can be quite effective in *persuasive* messages set up with the indirect approach. You can build up to your most important reason; then the *last* item your reader sees just before your suggestion or recommendation is your *most* important (strongest) reason. Here's an example.

TO:      Roger Hewitt
FROM:   Marilyn Hobbs
SUBJECT: Word Processing Units

As you know, our project managers dictate most of their routine reports. At present, each report must be dictated in its entirety. This process is very time-consuming. It's also quite repetitious since 50 to 60 percent of each report contains information that repeats standard information common to each project.

We could cut this time and eliminate most of the repetitious dictation if we connected word processing units to our Premex 250 computer. Our routine, repetitive reports could be stored in the computer. Then our managers would only have to dictate the new material. The transcriber could recall the stored report from the computer onto the word processor and insert the additional information.

Transcription time would be reduced by at least 40 percent, perhaps more, thus relieving the overtime situation in that section and bringing our payroll costs back into line.

Our project managers could spend more time on project control and less time on routine paperwork. In addition, the quality of their reports may improve, since they would only dictate significant information.

Best of all, we already have a computer with adequate storage capacity and three word processing transcribers that we've never used to their full capabilities. The initial cost of the word processing units would be quickly offset.

I recommend that we purchase word processing units during this quarter. A detailed cost breakdown is enclosed.

### Problem/Cause/Solution Sequence

This sequence should be used when it's necessary to explain a problem and recommend a solution. You can use this sequence on any problem, even though you don't have the solution worked out, because it's a *logical* way to discuss a problem.

The sequence works this way: (1) define the problem, (2) analyze or explain the cause(s), and (3) recommend the solution(s). Defining the problem adequately is very important because you must convince your reader that you're solving a worthwhile problem. If your reader doesn't "see" the problem before you begin to analyze its causes, your analysis and solution won't make much sense. How much "definition" is necessary depends on your reader, of course. In the example below, the problem can be defined quickly.

TO:      W. C. Wilson
FROM:   J. R. Rosenbloom
SUBJECT: Excess Humidity in the Computer Room

Excessive moisture in the air can cause our computers to malfunction. Recently, the humidity level in the machine room has frequently risen higher than the acceptable limit, and our machines have malfunctioned.

After analyzing several possible causes, we've determined that the new automatic door from the machine room into the west hallway fails to close properly after medium to heavy use. When more than four or five people use the door in rapid succession, the door stays open, letting in the warm air from the west hallway. Sometimes the open door is noticed, but usually the situation isn't discovered until the humidity level has risen to an unacceptable level. If you recall, the door is at the end of a long hallway, just out of sight of our machine room people.

Now that we have determined the cause, our people are more aware of the sticking door and check it frequently. But we need a better solution.

I recommend we replace the present door with a Triway Model 235, which is much sturdier and has a heavy-duty automatic mechanism. The cost is about one-third more than what we paid for the present door, but we can easily regain the difference through increased machine time. A cost analysis is enclosed.

Let me know if you need additional information. We need to solve this problem quickly.

### Comparison/Contrast Sequence

Two or more items (ideas, machines, solutions, etc.) can be compared using this sequence. Sometimes this sequence is linked up with the advantages/disadvantages sequence, but it isn't always necessary to discuss advantages and disadvantages when comparing items. Here's a comparison of leasing costs to purchasing costs for a batch of electronic typewriters.

TO:       Henry Dubinsky
FROM:   Walter Patroni
SUBJECT: Cost Analysis of Quintex and Easywrite
           Electronic Typewriters

As you requested, we've compared leasing costs to purchasing costs for eight Quintex and eight Easywrite electronic typewriters.

Leasing eight Quintex machines for three years will cost $28,450, including maintenance. Purchasing the machines will cost $24,675. A separate maintenance contract with Quintex would cost $1,575, bringing the total to $26,250. Thus, outright purchase would save us $2,200.

On the other hand, leasing eight Easywrite typewriters for three years will cost $27,150, including maintenance. Purchasing these machines will cost $23,500, which includes a one-year maintenance contract. An additional two years' maintenance would cost $875, bringing the total to $24,375. In this case, outright purchase would save us $2,775.

Purchasing either the Quintex or Easywrite machines is less expensive than leasing. In addition, purchasing Easywrites will save us $575. However, before we make our final decision, I suggest we talk to Jane O'Brien about the capital equipment expenditure budget.

### Advantages/Disadvantages Sequence

This sequence is closely related to the comparison/contrast sequence, except you're specifically comparing advantages to disadvantages. Moreover, you don't need two or more items. For example, you could list the advantages and disadvantages of installing a new system or buying a new piece of machinery. You can also use this sequence to evaluate a job applicant, as Leroy Newsome does in the following memo. This sequence is also called the "reasons for/reasons against" or "plus/minus" sequence.

TO:        Sarah Jorgenson
FROM:      Leroy Newsome
SUBJECT:   William Stoner

I interviewed William Stoner yesterday at the Hodges Hotel.

Mr. Stoner is a well-qualified candidate. He has a master's degree in accounting from Western State University and seven years of experience in general accounting. He's presently director of accounting systems for Nortrell Digitonics in Crafton. I know several people at Nortrell, and they've always spoken highly of him.

However, though his management experience is excellent, most of his accounting background is in general accounting. He has had very little exposure to cost accounting. In addition, he's somewhat reluctant to relocate to our area.

We need a heavyweight in cost accounting, preferably someone with a strong background in manufacturing systems. Although Mr. Stoner's record is impressive, I think we should pass because of his weak cost experience.

### Negative/Positive Sequence

This sequence is used when it's necessary to convey negative or controversial information while still maintaining your reader's good will. The sequence works this way: (1) mention the situation, (2) provide details or an explanation, (3) give the negative information, (4) suggest a workable alternative if possible, and (5) close with a positive statement.

The idea behind the sequence is to *close* on a positive note if possible, because that's the last thing your reader will see. If you reveal all of your positive information immediately, then your message is all downhill after that. Of course, the *ideal way* to use this sequence is to "sandwich" your negative message between two positive pieces of information.

TO:         Willard Harrison
FROM:       Joanna Martinez
SUBJECT: Work-at-Home Program

I've read your report recommending that we hire full-time employees to do work at home. I agree that there are substantial advantages in the work-at-home program, particularly for the employees.

However, I have a few questions. What about the local zoning regulations that might restrict or prohibit employment in the home? Also, how do we handle job-related accidents that occur in the home? What is the employee's responsibility for damaged equipment? These questions and others need to be answered before we can commit ourselves to this program.

In addition, your recommended program covers only full-time employees. In our business I think that we would probably want to start with part-time employees. I think you would be on much stronger ground with a part-time program, especially since this is such a new concept for us. Why don't you work up some ideas for a part-time program?

Your report is good, and it breaks some important ground, but why not take another look at the program from a slightly different perspective?

Now we've covered the entire process to *develop your overall plan* for your letter, memo, or report. Here are the five steps again:

1. *Determine* your purpose for writing. (*Why* am I writing this letter/memo/report/etc.?)
2. *Choose* an overall approach. (*Which* overall approach should I use?)
3. *Decide* what information your opening should contain. (*What* information should my opening contain?)
4. *Decide* what information your "closing" should contain. (*What* information should my closing contain?)

5. *Select* an organizational sequence for your "body." (*Which* organizational sequence should I use for my body?)

Let's apply this process to the Work-at-Home Program memo we just looked at.

**1. Question: Why am I writing this memo?**

Answer: (*Primary purpose*) To tell Willard Harrison that his "work-at-home" report isn't complete and doesn't address our major interest (part-time employees).

(*Secondary purpose*) To encourage Willard to focus on a program for part-time employees.

**2. Question: Which overall approach should I use?**

Answer: (*Indirect approach*) Because I want Willard to read my explanation *before* he finds out his recommendation won't be accepted.

**3. Question: What information should my opening contain?**

Answer: (*Introduce the subject*) Work-at-Home recommendations.

**4. Question: What information should my closing contain?**

Answer: (*Tell the decision*) We're more interested in a part-time program. (*Ask for action*) Encourage Willard to work up a part-time program.

**5. Question: Which organizational sequence should I use for my body?**

Answer: (*Negative/positive sequence*) Since I want to close by asking Willard to do something positive (look at a part-time program), my negative message should come first (mention the incomplete information and that the report covers full-time only). Then I can suggest a possible alternative (look at a part-time program) and close with a positive statement (good report; take another look).

Although it has taken me three chapters to explain this process, developing your overall plan is simply a matter of asking and answering five questions and writing a few short notes to yourself. I'm sure *my* "notes" to answer the five questions are more elaborate than the notes you would write to yourself because you would be using your own form of shorthand, key words, etc. However, the more you use this process, the more proficient you'll become. In a very short time, you'll discover that organizing your material has become easier and can be accomplished more quickly.

*Exercises*

1. Here's one of the memos from this chapter for you to analyze by answering these questions (underline the words and phrases that support your answers):

    a. What is the *purpose* of this memo?
    b. Which *overall approach* is used?
    c. What *type of information* does the opening contain?
    d. What *type of information* does the closing contain?
    e. Which *organizational sequence* is used in the body?

TO:       Sarah Jorgenson
FROM:   Leroy Newsome
SUBJECT: William Stoner

I interviewed William Stoner yesterday at the Hodges Hotel.

    Mr. Stoner is a well-qualified candidate. He has a master's degree in accounting from Western State University and seven years of experience in general accounting. He's presently director of accounting systems for Nortrell Digitonics in Crafton. I know several people at Nortrell, and they've always spoken highly of him.

However, though his management experience is excellent, most of his accounting background is in general accounting. He has had very little exposure to cost accounting. In addition, he's somewhat reluctant to relocate to our area.

We need a heavyweight in cost accounting, preferably someone with a strong background in manufacturing systems. Although Mr. Stoner's record is impressive, I think we should pass because of his weak cost experience.

2. Assume you have been asked to write a report on each of the following subjects. Which organizational sequence is the most appropriate for each of these subjects? Pick only one for each question.

    a. chronological (sequential) sequence
    b. priority sequence
    c. reverse priority sequence
    d. problem/cause/solution sequence
    e. comparison/contrast sequence
    f. advantages/disadvantages sequence
    g. negative/positive sequence

1. _____ You're the official recording secretary for an organization and must write a report after each meeting.
2. _____ You've been asked to examine how three companies solved the same problem.
3. _____ You've been asked to provide a breakdown of your department's activities.
4. _____ You're asked to write a set of instructions for operating a piece of machinery.
5. _____ You've been sent to a meeting to gather information for your boss.
6. _____ You're asked to evaluate a new employee relations program before it's put into effect.

7. _____ You're asked to find out why employees don't read your company's manuals and recommend some changes.

8. _____ You're responsible for determining what items should be purchased for your office.

9. _____ You're asked to examine two pieces of machinery and determine which ones will cost less to operate.

10. _____ You're asked to find out what's wrong with the office air-conditioning system.

*Answers to Exercises*

1. a. *Primary Purpose:* To explain to Sarah Jorgenson why I've concluded that William Stoner shouldn't be hired.
*Secondary purpose:* To inform Sarah of Mr. Stoner's qualifications.

b. *Indirect Approach:* Because I want Sarah to understand *how* I evaluated Mr. Stoner *before* I concluded we shouldn't hire him.

c. *Introduce the Subject:* "I interviewed William Stoner...."

d. *Conclusion:* " ... need ... heavyweight ... cost accounting ... with ... manufacturing systems...."
*Recommendation:* " ... pass because ... his weak cost experience."

e. *Advantages/Disadvantages Sequence:*

*Advantages:* " ... well-qualified...." " ... master's degree in accounting ... seven years of experience...." " ... director ... accounting systems...." "... several people ... spoken highly of him." " ... management experience ... excellent...."

*Disadvantages:* " ... most ... accounting background ... general accounting." " ... very little ... cost accounting." " ... reluctant to relocate...."

**2.** 1. chronological (sequential) sequence (a)
2. comparison/contrast sequence (e)
3. priority sequence (b)
4. chronological (sequential) sequence (a)
5. priority sequence (b)
6. advantages/disadvantages sequence (f)
7. problem/cause/solution sequence (d)
8. priority sequence (b)
9. comparison/contrast sequence (e)
10. problem/cause/solution sequence (d)

# CHAPTER TWELVE

# Punctuate Appropriately

To some people, punctuation rules seem mysterious and full of exceptions that must be mastered. Yet with the possible exception of the comma, most *major* punctuation uses are straightforward and can be learned very quickly.

For example, if you know only one major use of the semicolon (to separate complete sentences) and one major use of the colon (to introduce a series or list), you can punctuate most sentences that require semicolons and colons. The other uses of the semicolon and colon are needed less frequently and can often be avoided if you're not sure of their proper usages.

Thus, you can master the *most important* semicolon and colon uses in just a few minutes, and you'll use them "correctly" most of the time. All punctuation (dashes, quotation marks, apostrophes, etc.) can be approached this way: Learn the *most important* usages and forget the exceptions and infrequent uses that make punctuation rules seem so confusing.

It's important to master these major punctuation uses because correct punctuation is essential to effective on-the-job writing. If we punctuate our sentences appropriately, our readers won't have to figure out what we mean or mentally substitute the correct punctuation.

Here's a confusing sentence that results from using a comma incorrectly:

I went to work, however, I should've stayed home because I was still sick.

The confusion occurs because the word "however" can be attached to *either* the first part of the sentence *or* the second part:

> I went to work, however. I should've stayed home because I was still sick.

> I went to work. However, I should've stayed home because I was still sick.

Complete clarity can be achieved by applying semicolon rule 2 (to separate complete sentences joined by conjunctive adverbs, e.g., "however," "consequently," "therefore").

> I went to work; however, I should've stayed home because I was still sick.

> I went to work, however; I should've stayed home because I was still sick.

Let's look at a few punctuation rules. The *major uses* of the comma (,), semicolon (;), colon(:), dash (—), apostrophe ('), and quotation marks ("" '') can be summarized quickly. There are other uses, of course, and other punctuation marks, but becoming familiar with the major uses and the major marks will keep your punctuation "correct" most of the time.

First, though, here are a few short definitions that will make it easier to follow the discussion:

*Independent clause:* a complete sentence that can stand by itself.

> Richard decided to buy an additional two hundred shares of stock.

*Dependent clause:* a part of a sentence that can't stand by itself; it must be helped by an independent clause.

> *Although he had been unwise in his previous purchases*, Richard decided to buy an additional two hundred shares of stock.

*Nonrestrictive clause:* additional information about a part of a sentence.

> Dr. Williams, *who is our personal physician*, arrived late last night.

*Coordinating conjunction:* a transitional word that connects two independent clauses; the word has a fixed position between the independent clauses it connects.

> The carpenters arrived late, *but* they finished the job on time.

Other coordinating conjunctions are *and, nor, or, for.*

*Conjunctive adverb:* a transitional word that doesn't have a fixed position in a sentence.

> We need many items for the office; *however,* our funds are limited.
> We need many items for the office; our funds, *however,* are limited.
> We need many items for the office; our funds are limited, *however.*

Other conjunctive adverbs are *also, anyway, besides, consequently, finally, furthermore, hence, incidentally, indeed, instead, likewise, meanwhile, moreover, nevertheless, next, otherwise, still, subsequently, then, therefore, thus.*

### Comma (,)

We'll start with the comma because it's the most difficult. Once you've mastered the major uses of the comma, the other punctuation uses will seem easier.

> 1. *To separate independent clauses (complete sentences) joined by a coordinating conjunction (and, but, for, nor, or):*
>
> > The new magazine wasn't gaining adequate subscriptions, and the editor feared that a significant number of reporters would need to be laid off.

Erratic stock prices worried the potential investors, but the merger proposal passed unanimously.

2. *After a dependent clause (not complete sentence) that precedes an independent clause:*

After months of cutting operating expenses, the company was forced to close permanently.

If employee morale is consistently low, productivity will be affected.

3. *To set off a nonrestrictive clause (additional information):*

The town of Clermont, which is located near Gainesville, dedicated a statue to General Horace McGee, Clermont's founding father.

Agnes Wilson, who is our regional sales manager, will call on you next week.

4. *To separate words, phrases, or clauses in a series:*

Representatives from Missouri, Illinois, and Kentucky attended the marketing seminar.

The instructor introduced herself, gave a brief explanation of the course, and passed out the course outline.

5. *To set off transitional words and expressions (in short, of course) or conjunctive adverbs (however, consequently, therefore):*

Our consultant, however, disagreed with the committee's decision.

All Mrs. Hearnes was interested in, of course, was making her point.

Unfortunately, soaring mortgage rates have kept

many young couples from buying their dream houses.

6. *To separate two or more adjectives that modify the same noun*:

Young doctors are accustomed to long, sleepless nights during their residency.

John's firm, straightforward, no-nonsense approach to the problem impressed his boss.

7. *To set off a short direct quotation*:

The instructor said, "Please pass your tests forward."

Dr. Simpson warned Mr. Tate, "Quit smoking or I can't help you."

8. *After expressions that introduce an example or illustration*:

For example, some generic drugs work just as well as the brand-name drugs.

For instance, many cities, such as Crenshaw, Hillsdale, and Fayville, have curfew laws.

9. *To separate two words that might otherwise be misunderstood*:

Instead of fifteen, twenty came.

To Billy, Joe was always a friend.

10. *To set off items in dates, addresses, names of places*:

The conference on energy conservation will be held October 10 at 236 Gleason Drive, Summitville, Wisconsin.

Joanna was born on June 25, 1958, at 168 Terrance Road, Winston, North Dakota.

### Semicolon (;)

*1. To separate independent clauses (complete sentences) that aren't joined by a coordinating conjunction (and, but, for, nor, or):*

Mrs. Lawrence studied our production line last month; she was pleased with our innovations.

Our computer broke down late last night; it wasn't repaired until noon today.

*2. To separate independent clauses joined by conjunctive adverbs (however, consequently, therefore):*

Afternoon showers were predicted for Saturday; consequently, the outdoor symphony performance was held indoors.

Printers at Acme Press tested a new printing machine last week; however, they still prefer the older machine to the newer model.

*3. To separate clauses containing commas that could be confusing:*

The following people attended the budget meeting: John Burns, manager, payroll; Susan Heller, supervisor, personnel; Wilma Knight, manager, administrative services; and David Gomez, assistant supervisor, facilities management.

### Colon (:)

*1. To introduce a series or list:*

Four items are on the agenda for tomorrow's meeting: employee relations, office facilities, accounting methods, and vacation schedules.

State University offers the following foreign languages: French, German, Spanish, and Russian.

2. *To introduce material in a formal manner (notice that the material is expressed in a complete sentence)*:

A question came up for discussion: Which labor relations policy should be followed?

The pamphlet on vitamins presented an interesting piece of information: The body reacts exactly the same to synthetic vitamins as it does to natural vitamins.

### Dash (—)

1. *To emphasize material in a sentence*:

Two radio stations—KLUP and KNKO—carried extensive coverage of the hotel fire.

Machine malfunctions—which occur daily—are costing the company over $13,000 a month.

2. *To indicate a summarizing statement (notice that the summary statement after the dash is a complete sentence)*:

Lipstick, nail lacquer, and mascara—these are just three of the many items Sparkle Cosmetics manufactures.

Poor workmanship, inferior materials, and failure to meet deadlines—these were the main reasons for our drastic sales decline.

### Apostrophe (')

1. *To form the possessive case of nouns and some pronouns:*

> the woman's dress; the boy's bicycle; a year's delay; someone's tennis shows; Gretchen's house.

2. *To indicate the omission of figures or letters:*

> shouldn't (should not); it's (it is); there's (there is); class of '63 (1963); you're (you are).

3. *To form the plural of letters, figures, and symbols:*

> the 1980's; three R's; 4 by 6's; cross the t's; 5's.

### Double Quotation Marks ("")

1. *To enclose direct quotations:*

> "Are you sure," asked Alex, "that you understand the seriousness of your accusation?"

> "George, why didn't you come to the concert last night?" Susan asked.

2. *To enclose titles of speeches, lectures, articles, short stories, short poems, radio and TV programs (note: titles of books, long poems, and full-length motion pictures are usually underlined or italicized):*

> Robert Samoza will speak on "Investment Opportunities" tonight at the Lexington Auditorium.

> We watched a program called "Success in Business."

3. *To enclose coined words, or ordinary words used ironically or for emphasis:*

In short, I don't think the committee's "recommendation" is quite what we expected.

Most people want to avoid another "cold war."

George Herman "Babe" Ruth hit 60 home runs in one season.

### Single Quotation Marks (' ')

1. *To enclose another quotation within a direct quotation*:

My boss told me, "Make sure you attend the 'Economics Is Fun' lecture next week."

One critic stated, "Ernest Hemingway's story 'The Short Happy Life of Francis Macomber' contains a good example of the 'macho' hunter."

You can master these punctuation rules by studying each rule for just a few minutes. However, for an even quicker way to improve your punctuation, learn *comma* rules 1, 2, and 3, *semicolon* rules 1 and 2, and *colon* rule 1. These six rules will cover many types of sentences you're likely to write and provide an adequate variety in your punctuation uses.

*Exercises*
Punctuate the following sentences:

1. All the crew members finished their assignments before the deadline Mrs. Rath was very pleased.

2. Ms. Thomas who is our interior decorator met with Mr. Farrone yesterday.

3. I told him to speak out out of turn if necessary.

4. The executive council includes the following people John Richards manager administration Jane Flynn supervisor accounts payable Warren Henderson assistant manager accounts receivable Joan Fields vice-

president marketing and Phil Gonzales executive vice-president.

5. My office needs a rug new drapes and a lamp but my budget will only permit the purchase of a lamp.

6. This years contract should be everybodys concern but it isnt.

7. We learn responsibility in three ways by example by instruction and by experience.

8. We were late arriving at the airport however we didn't miss our plane.

9. Fill in all the blanks on the application form Mrs. Golden said before you hand in the form.

10. My father he is the president of the company will call this matter to the attention of the board of directors.

11. After youve read the quarterly report youll understand why we lost money.

12. Our company has several well-known products several of them have been in existence since the 1950s.

13. After we had finished eating our stomachs were upset.

14. True vegetarians eat no meat dairy products or processed foods.

15. The strikers in short attracted a large group of supporters.

16. Inclement weather inadequate parking facilities and poor booth arrangement kept the crowds small and profits low at the art festival.

17. Both parties involved in the merger agreed on one point the companies management would remain the same.

18. Many airlines Consolidated Northern Chartwell offer discount fares for night travelers.

19. Mr. Lewis announced to our investment group Karen Green the noted economist will lecture tonight on Investing for the Future at Willis Auditorium 608 Phelps Street.

20. I thought he was from Millerville Kansas but his birth certificate indicates he was born in Tyler Arkansas on June 15 1954.

## *Answers to Exercises*

1. All the crew members finished their assignments before the deadline; Mrs. Rath was very pleased.

All the crew members finished their assignments before the deadline. Mrs. Rath was very pleased.

2. Ms. Thomas, who is our interior decorator, met with Mr. Farrone yesterday.

3. I told him to speak out, out of turn, if necessary. (Or comma after "turn" may be omitted.)

4. The executive council includes the following people: John Richards, manager, administration; Jane Flynn, supervisor, accounts payable; Warren Henderson, assistant manager, accounts receivable; Joan Fields, vice-president, marketing; and Phil Gonzales, executive vice-president.

5. My office needs a rug, new drapes, and a lamp, but my budget will only permit the purchase of a lamp.

6. This year's contract should be everybody's concern, but it isn't.

7. We learn responsibility in three ways: by example, by instruction, and by experience.

8. We were late arriving at the airport; however, we didn't miss our plane.

9. "Fill in all the blanks on the application form," Mrs. Golden said, "before you hand in the form."

10. My father—he is the president of the company—will call this matter to the attention of the board of directors.

11. After you've read the quarterly report, you'll understand why we lost money.

12. Our company has several well-known products; several of them have been in existence since the 1950's.

13. After we had finished eating, our stomachs were upset.

14. True vegetarians eat no meat, dairy products, or processed foods.

15. The strikers, in short, attracted a large number of supporters.

16. Inclement weather, inadequate parking facilities, and poor booth arrangement kept the crowds small and the profits low at the art festival.

17. Both parties involved in the merger agreed on one point: the companies' management would remain the same.

18. Many airlines—Consolidated, Northern, Chartwell—offer discount fares for night travelers.

19. Mr. Lewis announced to our investment group, "Karen Green, the noted economist, will lecture tonight on 'Investing for the Future' at Willis Auditorium, 608 Phelps Street."

20. I thought he was from Millerville, Kansas, but his birth certificate indicates he was born in Tyler, Arkansas, on June 15, 1954.

# CHAPTER THIRTEEN

# Spell Correctly

Poor spelling can be embarrassing. No matter how much we would like to believe it doesn't matter, or how many excuses we make, poor spelling brands a person as either "poorly educated" or "too lazy" (or uncaring) to catch and correct the mistakes.

Regardless of how well you write, poor spelling can hurt your personal image, tarnish your "business" image, and interfere with your message's effectiveness.

This chapter isn't a primer on spelling, but it will help you discover whether you're a poor speller and give you some ideas to correct the problem. Many people think they're poor spellers, when in reality the number of words they misspell in their daily vocabulary is small or limited. The frequent repetition of these misspelled words makes their spelling problem appear greater than it really is. If you have difficulty with spelling, try a few of the ideas in this chapter before giving up or labeling yourself a poor speller for life.

First, let's take a spelling test. The twenty-five words below are often misspelled. I've listed the correctly spelled word with the most frequent misspellings. Pick out the correct word.

1. accidently, accidentally
2. admittence, admittance, admitance, admitence
3. believable, beleiveable, believeable
4. business, bussiness, bussines, busines
5. clientle, clientel, clientele
6. deceive, decieve
7. definately, definitely, defintly, definitly, definatly
8. disappoint, dissapoint, dissappoint, disapoint
9. efficiency, efficency, eficiency, efficiancy

10. excede, exceed, exceede
11. familar, familiar, famliar, famaliar
12. independant, independint, independent
13. leisure, liesure
14. maintanence, maintenence, maintenance
15. neccesary, necessary, neccessary
16. occasionally, occasionaly, ocassionally, occassionly, occassionally
17. occurance, ocurrence, occurrance, occurence, occurrence
18. permanant, permenant, permanent, permenent
19. persistent, persistant, pursistent, pursistant
20. perferred, perfered, prefered, preferred
21. questionnaire, questionaire
22. recieve, receive
23. recomend, reccomend, recommend, reccommend
24. separately, separtly, seperately, sepertly
25. witholding, withholding, witholdding

The above words are used so often in on-the-job writing that misspelling even a few of them is bound to project a poor image. Here are the correct spellings:

1. accidentally 2. admittance 3. believable 4. business 5. clientele 6. deceive 7. definitely 8. disappoint 9. efficiency 10. exceed 11. familiar 12. independent 13. leisure 14. maintenance 15. necessary 16. occasionally 17. occurrence 18. permanent 19. persistent 20. preferred 21. questionnaire 22. receive 23. recommend 24. separately 25. withholding

If you had problems with some of these words, write them down. These could be words that you write every day. If you do use them frequently, you should devise a method to learn how to spell them. Misspelling these words every time will make your spelling appear worse than it may be.

Here are a few suggestions to help you improve your spelling:

1. *Perform an analysis* to determine the words you misspell most often. Go over several of your letters/memos/reports/etc., and circle each misspelled word. Or have someone else go through your material.

2. *Keep a list* of misspelled words. Notice how many times you misspell the *same* word or words. Pick out the *most frequently misspelled words* and put them on another list. You may be surprised; the list might not be as long as you think. We all use certain words over and over again. If these words happen to be the ones you misspell most often, you're projecting the image of a poor speller.

    If your list is five hundred words long, you have a deep-seated spelling problem that will take a lot of time and effort to correct. On the other hand, a twenty-five word list can be tackled quickly and effectively.

3. *Master the spelling* of the most frequently misspelled words. These words may be difficult for you, but they can be mastered. Use any method that works for you. Try writing the words over and over. Try writing the words on cards and studying them briefly several times a day. The idea is to become *conscious* of these words as *problem* words so that you'll be more cautious when you write them.

    If you're having trouble with words that sound as if they should have the same ending (*familiar/similar*), try memorizing only *one* of the words. For example, if you memorize "familiar," you can always spell "similar" by telling yourself, "That's the word I *didn't* memorize, but I know it's *different* from the word I did memorize."

    Or find other words *within* words that can help you remember the spelling. For instance, there's "a rat" in *separate;* There's a "liar" in fam*iliar*; and there's only one "bus" in *bus*iness.

These ideas may sound crazy, but sometimes they work. Despite all the spelling rules, learning to spell isn't always a "scientific" process.

4. *Use a dictionary* as often as necessary, even if you're looking up the same word over and over.

Many poor spellers are lazy. They "suspect" that certain words aren't spelled correctly, but they don't take the time to look them up. You should always consult a dictionary if you're not sure about a word. If you don't have the slightest idea how to find a word, get someone to help you. Word guides (35,000 words spelled and divided, etc.) are also valuable tools. Dictionaries for poor spellers may be a bit more expensive, but they list words by their common misspellings and give the correct spellings.

Even good spellers look up words in dictionaries to double-check spellings. Very few people are perfect spellers, although the finished letter, memo, or report may be perfect.

5. *Get a spelling handbook* and learn one spelling rule a week.

After you've come up with your misspelled word list, you'll probably notice that you misspell words that have similar patterns. Be especially alert for misspelled words that have these patterns:

| | |
|---|---|
| *ie* and *ei* | achieve, believe; deceive, receive |
| *ance* and *ence* | assistance, resistance; existence, insistence |
| *ant* and *ent* | dominant, dormant; permanent, prominent |
| *able* and *ible* | advisable, reliable; destructible, sensible |
| *ary* and *ery* | boundary, customary; cemetery, gallery |

| | |
|---|---|
| *ize* and *ise* | criticize, emphasize; advertise, supervise |
| *ceed* and *cede* | proceed, succeed; precede, recede |

Without performing your own "spelling analysis," you'll never know what your particular spelling problems are. Zero in on your problems and learn the rules *one by one.* Don't attempt to tackle everything at once (or in large doses). It's too easy to become discouraged. Work with one rule and certain groups of words until you feel you've mastered them.

Learn the *easy* rules first; then take on the tougher ones. For example, *almost* all English words that begin with "q" are followed by "u" (*quality, quantity, qualify, quandary,* etc.). Any spelling rule that applies to virtually all words should be the first one you master. It's the exception that makes spelling (and punctuation) so confusing.

6. *Proofread* every letter, memo, and report you write.

If you have time, put your document aside and come back to it later. "Cold" reading is an excellent way to catch spelling errors. Whatever proofreading method you use, if a word doesn't "look right," look it up in your dictionary or word guide. Many people are "print-oriented"; they can *recognize* misspelled words by the way the words "look" on the paper. They still may not be able to spell the doubtful words, but their spelling "suspicions" have become aroused, and they look up the words. If you are print-oriented, take advantage of these "tip-offs."

In fact, by necessity, this chapter has been geared toward print-oriented spellers. If you've been able to *recognize* the misspelled words (even though you can't spell the words correctly without your dictionary), you're probably print-oriented. If so, don't ignore these "red flags."

7. *Pronounce* your words carefully.

Reading *aloud* is an excellent proofreading technique. Pronouncing the words forces you to slow down and doesn't allow your "silent eye" to *anticipate* the words (more about the "silent eye" in Chapter Fourteen). In addition, some people are "audio-oriented"; they spell words by *sound* instead of *sight*.

Unfortunately, audio-oriented spellers who don't carefully pronounce their words misspell words frequently. And since audio-oriented spellers rely more heavily on "hearing" than "seeing" words, they're at the mercy of other people who don't pronounce words carefully.

Here are a few words that are often misspelled because audio-oriented spellers either hear or pronounce the words incorrectly:

| Misspelled | Correct |
|---|---|
| athelete, atholete | athlete |
| controversey | controversy |
| definately | definitely |
| equipted | equipped |
| incidently | incidentally |
| maintanence | maintenance |
| mathmatics | mathematics |
| prompness | promptness |
| quanity | quantity |
| sophmore | sophomore |

An audio-oriented speller reading these misspelled words won't necessarily "see" the mistakes. A print-oriented speller will probably at least *recognize* that something is wrong with the words.

If you're an audio-oriented speller who has spelling problems, try working on your spelling (and pronunciation) by using a cassette tape recorder. Using your spelling list, pronounce each word carefully and distinctly as you record it. As you record, pause a few seconds between each word so that later you'll have enough time to write down each word as it's played back. Or let someone else read your spelling list into the recorder. Pick someone who speaks clearly and distinctly. Then play back your tape and try to spell the words correctly.

Of course, if you're a print-oriented speller, you can also use this technique, as well as the other methods discussed in this chapter. At work, however, you may have more success by reading your words *aloud* to slow down your reading speed and give your "print-oriented eye" a better chance to catch the errors.

But remember, you have to take advantage of your "eye" and look up those doubtful words.

### Exercises

1. Circle and correct all misspelled words in the following sentences:

a. Our healthy third-quarter earnings significantly improved our companie's chances of persauding our lenders to renew their financial package.

b. Please take the appropriate action to make sure we gain controling interest in the new company.

c. It's advantagous for us to procede with the plan we've already set up.

d. Her diligence finally won her a promotion to computor operations manager.

e. His handwriting is nearly illegible, but he becomes extremely irritable if anyone mentions it to him.

f. If you'll follow the proper precedures, you'll be able to acheive immediate results.

g. Our hosery department carries many miscelleneous items.

h. The committee voted unanimously to recind our policy committment.

i. His negligance in this matter has led to several undesireable results.

j. After working hours, the vault will be accessable only under extraordinery circumstances.

2. Here are another forty commonly misspelled words in letters, memos, and reports. Circle and correct all misspelled words.

| | |
|---|---|
| 1) abscence _____ | 21) fourty _____ |
| 2) accumulate _____ | 22) grieveous _____ |
| 3) acoustics _____ | 23) harrass _____ |
| 4) admissable _____ | 24) indispensible _____ |
| 5) auditer _____ | 25) knowledgable _____ |
| 6) brillant _____ | 26) liason _____ |
| 7) bulliten _____ | 27) mediocre _____ |
| 8) catagory _____ | 28) negotiable _____ |
| 9) collateral _____ | 29) noticeable _____ |
| 10) competiter _____ | 30) ommision _____ |
| 11) convienent _____ | 31) paralell _____ |
| 12) diaphram _____ | 32) personel _____ |
| 13) disaproval _____ | 33) posesses _____ |
| 14) disbursemant _____ | 34) priviledge _____ |
| 15) discipline _____ | 35) persue _____ |
| 16) discrepency _____ | 36) restuarant _____ |
| 17) distribtor _____ | 37) saleable _____ |
| 18) embarassing _____ | 38) tangable _____ |
| 19) endorsement _____ | 39) truely _____ |
| 20) exagerate _____ | 40) vaccum _____ |

*Answers to Exercises*

1. a. company's, persuading b. controlling c. advantageous, proceed d. computer e. no spelling errors f. procedures, achieve g. hosiery, miscellaneous h. rescind, commitment i. negligence, undesirable j. accessible, extraordinary

2. 1) absence 2) correct 3) correct 4) admissible 5) auditor 6) brilliant 7) bulletin 8) category 9) correct 10) competi-

tor 11) convenient 12) diaphragm 13) disapproval 14)
disbursement 15) correct 16) discrepancy 17) distribu-
tor 18) embarrassing 19) correct 20) exaggerate 21) forty
22) grievous 23) harass 24) indispensable 25) knowl-
edgeable 26) liaison 27) correct 28) correct 29) correct
30) omission 31) parallel 32) personnel 33) possesses
34) privilege 35) pursue 36) restaurant 37) salable 38)
tangible 39) truly 40) vacuum

# CHAPTER FOURTEEN

# Evaluate Your Writing

Evaluating our writing is a task most of us would prefer to ignore, yet it's an important step in effective on-the-job writing. We need to look at our letters, memos, and reports as communcation devices that can be evaluated for their effectiveness. And we need to gain some insight into our progress as writers. Are we getting better, worse, or what? Unless we devise some method to monitor our writing, it will be difficult to see where we've been, where we're going, and how far we've come.

Let's begin by summarizing the essential elements of effective on-the-job writing that should be applied to every letter, memo, or report you write:

| | |
|---|---|
| Planning | 20% |
| Writing | 25% |
| Revising | 45% |
| Evaluating | 10% |

These percentages will vary, of course, depending on the material, but you can see that *writing* and *revising* make up 70 percent of the total time usually spent in composing a letter, memo, or report. *Planning* and *evaluating* account for only 30 percent, yet, if you ignore these elements, your writing won't achieve full effectiveness.

As I've already discussed in Chapters Three, Nine, Ten, and Eleven, *planning* is often given far too little time in the writing process; we're always eager to plunge into the *writing* step to "get the job finished." Some people find *revising* to be a chore (if they revise at all), but *revising* is the heart of good writing (note the 45 percent). In Chapters Four, Five, Six, Seven, Eight, Twelve, and Thirteen, I've lumped the *writing* and *revising* steps together because it's difficult to discuss writing without actually *revising* writing samples. But these two steps are *separate* steps in the writing process. First drafts should rarely be sent out. *Revising* is the most important element of effective writing.

However, though *planning* and *revising* are often slighted in the writing process, *evaluating* usually never receives its mere 10 percent at all. We send off our letters, memos, and reports, and rarely follow up to determine whether they've achieved what we wanted. Yet, without evaluating our writing *before* and *after* we send our messages, we can't fully determine the effectiveness of our written communications.

Evaluating your writing involves doing at least three things:

Checking the overall image of each letter, memo, and report
Setting up an evaluation scale
Determining your writing weaknesses

### Check the Overall Image of Each Letter, Memo, and Report

Before you send any letter, memo, or report, you should *proofread* the final version and *check* its overall appearance. As I've mentioned before, "image" is important in on-the-job writing. Our written materials reflect how "professional" we are. If your material is poorly written or sloppy in appearance, your image will appear unprofessional, which can lead your reader to question the *value* of what you've written.

Here's an "image checklist" you can use before you send off your final version:

1. Is the *physical appearance* of your document "professional"?
   Are the margins and spacing correct?

Is the copy clean (free from smudges, dirt, etc.)?
Is the typed image dark enough?
Did you make effective use of headings, paragraphs, and white space to give your message an "inviting" appearance?

2. Is the message *organized* well?
Did you have an overall plan?
Did you follow your plan?
Do your ideas make sense? Are they logical?
Do you have a clearly defined opening, closing, and body?
Can you explain why you organized your message the way you did?

3. Is the message *written* well?
Is the wording correct?
Is the wording specific?
Is the wording concise?
Is the language appropriate for the reader?
Is there too much jargon?
Are the sentences as effective as you can make them?
Are the paragraphs set up correctly?
Is the message punctuated correctly?
Is the spelling correct?
Are there any missing words?

4. What is the *tone* of the message?
Is the tone tactful?
Is the tone positive, negative, or neutral?
Is the tone formal, informal, or conversational?
Is the overall tone "appropriate"?
Is the message "writer"- or "reader"- oriented?

### Set Up an Evaluation Scale

After you have sent your letter, memo, or report, you should follow up on it to determine its success. If you had a clearly defined purpose for writing, you should know what results or effects you expect. Of course, we can't always find out *everything* about the effectiveness of our messages, but we certainly shouldn't ignore valuable feedback from our readers.

One way to evaluate your effectiveness is to *set a standard* for your written communication and try to make sure that your writing meets your standard. You can set up an "evaluation scale" to measure your effectiveness. (See "Productive Potential Scale" on page 168.) Although the scale isn't "calibrated" or "scientific," it will give you an idea about the kind of standard you need to set.

I call this evaluation method the "productive potential scale" because I'm trying to determine ("measure") the effectiveness ("productivity") of my written communication. The scale is based on the following standard:

> My letter, memo, or report should accomplish my *primary purpose* for writing *without* additional written *or* oral communication to *correct* or *clarify* any omission(s) and/or misunderstanding(s).

Yes, it's a tough standard. If you adopt this standard for your written communication, few of your on-the-job documents will achieve +10. Even fewer will make it above +10. But consider how often we allow ourselves to make excuses for our nonproductive or counterproductive writing. Instead of finding out why some of our documents trigger phone calls for "additional information" or to "clarify a point," we let this "feedback" go unnoticed. It's easy to accept nonproductive and counterproductive written communication as part of "doing business."

In fact, one of the more popular activities in many organizations is a frustrating game called "memo tag." It works this way: I'll write you a memo that is incomplete in some manner; you'll write back asking for additional information; I'll write to you again, but I'll leave out something you need; you'll have to write again to ask for that something; then I'll write, etc., etc., etc.

---

## PRODUCTIVE POTENTIAL SCALE

---

| | | |
|---|---|---|
| Above + 10 | | Achieves <u>all</u> effects you wanted, without additional written or oral communication, and results in <u>additional benefits</u> for you and/or your organization. |
| | + 10 | Achieves <u>all</u> effects you wanted, without additional written or oral communication. |
| *Productive Written Communication* | + 5 | Achieves <u>most</u> effects you wanted, without additional written or oral communication. |
| | + 1 | Achieves <u>some</u> effects you wanted, without additional written or oral communication. |

---

| | | |
|---|---|---|
| *Nonproductive Written Communication* | 0 | Doesn't achieve any effects you wanted, but doesn't result in additional written or oral communication. |

---

| | | |
|---|---|---|
| | − 1 | Results in additional written or oral communication to correct/clarify a <u>minor</u> omission or misunderstanding. |
| *Counterproductive Written Communication* | − 5 | Results in a <u>substantial</u> or <u>complete</u> revision of the original document to correct/clarify <u>major</u> omissions and/or misunderstandings. |
| | − 10 | Results in a <u>series</u> of additional written and/or oral communications to correct/clarify omissions and/or misunderstandings. |
| Below − 10 | | Results in a <u>series</u> of additional written and/or oral communications that <u>never</u> correct/clarify the omissions and/or misunderstandings. |

---

Whole days, weeks, months, years, and careers can be built on "memo tag." It continues as long as management tolerates it and participates in it, but it's counterproductive. Sometimes, however, "memo tag" isn't played deliberately. Sometimes the participants genuinely don't understand how counterproductive their written communications have become.

If you're "explaining" your letters, memos, and reports on a regular basis, or if you're not receiving the results you want, you need an evaluation scale to monitor your "productivity." This scale can be adjusted, of course. Set a standard you can live with. The important thing is to start *evaluating* your written communication to determine your *progress* as you improve your writing. Using a scale permits you to "plug in numbers" so that you can keep track of your progress easily.

### Determine Your Writing Weaknesses

You should be able to use the techniques discussed in this book to analyze your writing to determine what your major weaknesses are. You can perform this analysis "selectively" or "piece by piece" by using the guidelines in each chapter as your yardsticks. But you can also obtain an "overview" of your writing problems by developing an evaluation method or "tool" to help you. The following step-by-step method is one way to analyze your writing. I'm sure you can modify it to fit *your* situation, but it will give you a few ideas.

1. *Gather a sample* of letters/memos/reports you've received from others.

2. *Reread* this material carefully. Divide it into two piles—Minus and Plus
      "MINUS" is writing you find difficult to understand, even after rereading it carefully, or writing you don't like, even if you're not sure why.

      "PLUS" is writing that is relatively easy to understand with careful reading, or writing that especially appeals to you.

3. *Determine why* the MINUS material is so difficult to understand or *why* it doesn't appeal to you. Write down these traits.

> If you find this difficult to do, reread the chapters on clarity (Chapter Four), jargon (Chapter Five), conciseness (Chapter Six), tone (Chapter Seven), and the organization material (Chapters Nine, Ten, Eleven).
>
> In addition, use your *own* words to describe these traits. You may not know why the writing is confusing or unclear to you, but at least you can identify the trait.

4. *Determine why* the PLUS material is easy to understand or *why* it appeals to you. Write down these traits.

> Again, you may find it helpful to review some of the chapters.

5. *Gather a sample* of *your* letters/memos/reports.

6. *Reread* your material. Divide it into two piles— MINUS and PLUS.

> Sometimes it's useful to read your material aloud because this slows down your reading speed. As pointed out in Chapter Thirteen (spelling), writing that was clear to the "silent eye" or "print-oriented eye" can become less clear when we actually pronounce the words. If you do find a difference in "clarity," your "silent eye" may be *anticipating* or *substituting* words, phrases, or meanings that are in your mind but not actually expressed in writing. Your reader, of course, can't "see" these words you meant to put down.

7. *Compare* your MINUS material to the MINUS traits you've identified in step 3.

8. *Compare* your PLUS material to the PLUS traits you've identified in step 4.

9. *Identify* any new MINUS and/or PLUS traits in your material that you didn't find in anyone else's material. Write down these traits.

10. *Improve* your writing by eliminating the MINUS traits.

> Sometimes identification of the problem(s) is all it takes to make you aware that you can improve your writing. Look for the *patterns* in your writing that occur frequently. We often feel that everything we write is poor or mediocre when, in fact, the problems are much less widespread. "Wordiness," for example, can make your writing long-winded, imprecise, and repetitious, yet wordiness can easily be corrected once you've identified the pattern.

> If you do find several MINUS traits in your writing, try working on *one at a time*, instead of tackling them all. Solving one problem at a time will encourage you to continue improving your writing because you'll see tangible results quickly.

These evaluation methods can help you analyze your writing weaknesses and work out a plan to improve your written communication. Evaluating your writing is an important final step in putting all the writing "pieces" together so that you can see your progress.

Well, we've gone through the planning, writing, revising, and evaluating stages rather quickly, but I think thoroughly enough for you to grasp the guidelines. I hope I've encouraged you to apply some or all of the shortcuts to your on-the-job written communication. I think you'll be surprised at how quickly your letters, memos, and reports can become more effective.

# Index

*Accordingly,* use of, 92
Action
    elaborating on, 121
    telling/requesting, 116-17, 119,
        120
Active vs. passive sentence
        patterns, 65
    exercises on, 69-70
Addition, words to indicate, 92
Addresses, punctuation of, 147-48
*Adjacent to,* use of, 92
Adjectives, punctuation for, 147
Advantages/disadvantages
        sequence, 135-36
Adverbs, conjunctive
    definition of, 145
    punctuation of, 146-47, 148
*Afterward,* use of, 92
*Also,* use of, 91, 92, 145
Ambiguous wording, 36-37
Analyses
    as openings or closings, 113
    *See also* Writing evaluation
*And,* use of, 92, 145
Angry tone, 77
*Anyway,* use of, 145
Apostrophes, rules for, 150
Appropriate tone, 22, 74-86
    checklist for, 166
    exercises on, 84, 86
Articles, punctuation for titles of,
        150
*As a result,* use of, 92
*As an illustration,* use of, 92
"Audio-oriented" people, 160-61
Authorization, mentioning the,
        114-15
Awkward language, 80

*Because of,* use of, 92
*Besides,* use of, 92, 145
*Beyond,* use of, 92
"Body"
    definition of, 128
    organization of, 101, 113,
        128-37
    exercises on, 139-42

Books, punctuation for titles of,
        150
Bureaucratic jargon, 47, 48-49,
        78
    exercises on, 56-59
*But,* use of, 91, 92, 145

"Cause/effect" method of
        developing paragraphs, 97
Channel in communications
        diagram, 21-22
Checklist for your writing, 165-66
Christie, Agatha, 5
Chronological sequence, 130-31
Clarity, 31-46
    ambiguous wording vs., 36-37
    correct word for, 32-34
    dangling sentence parts vs.,
        37-39
    exercises on, 44-46
    misplaced *which* and *that*
        clauses vs., 39-40
    "moveable" words and phrases
        vs., 40
    precise word for, 35-36
    sentence coordination for,
        40-42
    sentence logic for, 43-44
    straight order of ideas for,
        42-43
Clauses
    punctuation for, 145-46, 148
    types of, 144-45
    *which* and *that,* 39-40
Closings, 101, 112, 119-24
    definition of, 113
    exercises in, 125-26
Coined words, punctuation for,
        150-51
Colons
    rules for, 148-49
    use of, 143
Commas
    incorrect use of, 143-44
    rules for, 145-48
Common words, 53-54
    exercise on, 57

Communications process,
    diagram on, 21-22
Comparison
    in advantages/disadvantages
        sequence, 135-36
    words to indicate, 92
"Comparison/contrast" method of
    developing paragraphs, 96
Comparison/contrast sequence,
    134-35
Concise wording (opposite of
    wordiness), 22, 60-73, 171
    exercises on, 68-73
Conclusions
    drawing, 117, 119-20
    elaborating, 121
Conjunctions, coordinating
    definition of, 145
    punctuation for, 145-46
Conjunctive adverbs
    definition of, 145
    punctuation for, 146-47, 148
Consequently
    punctuation for, 146, 148
    use of, 145
Consequently so, use of, 92
Contractions
    apostrophes in, 150
    informal tone through, 81
    personal tone through, 76
Contrast
    sequence for, 134-35
    words to indicate, 92
Contrived language, 80
Conversely, use of, 92
Coordinating conjunctions
    definition of, 145
    punctuation for, 145-46
Corporate jargon, 47, 48-49
    exercises on, 56-59
Correct words, 32-34
    exercises on, 44
Counterproductive written
    communication, 168

Dashes, rules for, 149
Dates, punctuation of, 147-48
Decision
    elaborating on the, 121
    telling the, 116, 119

"Definition" method of developing
    paragraphs, 94-95
Dependent clauses
    definition of, 144
    punctuation for, 146
Details
    in "body" of document, 113
    unnecessary, 67-69
    exercises on, 70
Dictionaries, use of, 158, 159
Disadvantages, comparison
    sequence for, 135-36
Double meanings, 36-37
Double quotation marks, rules
    for, 150-51
Doublespeak, 48
Drawing conclusions, 117, 119-20
"Dummy" subjects, 63-64

Effectiveness
    in closings, 101, 112, 119-24
        exercises in, 125-26
    general exercises on, 9-20
    in openings, 101, 112-19
        exercises in, 125
    in paragraphs, 87-99
        developing paragraphs, 94-97
        exercises in, 97-99
        topic sentences, 87-89
        transitional devices, 89-94
    revising as most important
        element of, 165
Elaborating on the action/
    decision/conclusion/
    recommendation, 121
Emphasis
    dashes for, 149
    punctuation for words used for,
        150-51
Evaluation of your writing, 164-71
    checking overall image, 165-66
    determination of weaknesses,
        169-71
    percentage of time to be spent
        in, 164
    setting up scale, 166-69
"Example" method of developing
    paragraphs, 95
Examples
    punctuation for, 147

Examples, cont.
  words to indicate, 92
Exercises
  in appropriate tone, 84-86
  in conciseness, 69-73
  in effective paragraphs, 97-99
  in effective statements, 9-20
  vs. jargon, 56-59
  in planning, 109-11, 125-27,
    139-42
  punctuation, 151-54
  spelling, 161-63
  *See also* Quizzes
Explanation
  in "body" of document, 113
  words to indicate, 92


Feedback, 6, 7, 23, 167
Figures, punctuation for
  omissions, 150
  plurals, 150
*Finally,* use of, 91, 92, 145
*First, second, third,* use of, 91,
  92
*For,* use of, 145
*For example,* use of, 92
*For instance,* use of, 92
"Formal" writing, 80-82
  exercises on, 85
Further correspondence, making
  unnecessary, 121-22,
  167-69
*Furthermore,* use of, 92, 145


"General to specific" method of
  developing paragraphs, 96
General words, 34-35
Gobbledygook, 48
Goodwill message, using a,
  122-24
Graphs, 113


Hackneyed introductions to
  sentences, 62-63
*Hence,* use of, 92, 145
*However,*
  punctuation for, 146, 148
  use of, 91, 92, 145

*I would like to take the
  opportunity,* elimination of,
  62-63
Ideas, order of, 42-43
Illustrations, *see* Examples
Image of your writing, checking,
  165-66
Impersonal approach in letter-
  writing, 27-28
*In addition,* use of, 92
*In brief,* use of, 92
*In closing,* use of, 92
*In comparison,* use of, 92
*In contrast,* use of, 92
*In fact,* use of, 92
*In other words,* use of, 92
*In retrospect,* use of, 92
*In short,* use of, 92
*In turn,* use of, 92
Inappropriate tone, 22, 74-86
  checklist for, 166
  exercises on, 84-86
*Incidentally,* use of, 145
*Indeed,* use of, 145
Independent clauses
  definition of, 144
  punctuation of, 145-46, 148
"Inflated" words, 52-53, 78
  exercises on, 56-57
Informal tone, 80-82
  exercises for, 85
Information
  controversial, sequence for,
    136-37
  jargon and, 49
  providing background, 115-16
*Inside,* use of, 92
*Instead,* use of, 145
Interference, types of, 22, 31, 51
Introducing the subject, 113-14
Ironic words, punctuation for,
  150-51
*It has come to my attention,*
  elimination of, 63
*It is,* overuse of, 63-64, 79
Italics, use of, 150

Jargon, 22, 47-59
  bureaucratic (corporate), 47,
    48-49, 78

Jargon, cont.
    exercises on, 56-59
    technical, 47-48

Key words, 90-91

Lambuth, David, 50
*Later,* use of, 92
Latinistic vocabulary, 50
Lectures, punctuation for titles
    of, 150
Letters of the alphabet,
        punctuation for
    omissions, 150
    plurals, 150
*Likewise,* use of, 92, 145
"Listing" method of developing
    paragraphs, 94
Lists of words commonly
    misspelled, 155-56, 162
Logic of sentences, 43-44

Making further correspondence
    unnecessary, 121-22,
    167-69
Making recommendations,
    117-19, 120
*Meanwhile,* use of, 92, 145
"Memo tag," 168-69
Memoranda, five planning steps
    for, 138-39
Memorization of words frequently
    spelled, 157-58
Mentioning the authorization,
    114-15
Message in communication
    diagram, 21-22
*Moreover,* use of, 92, 145
Motion pictures, punctuation for
    titles of, 150
"Movable" words and phrases, 40
Movies, punctuation for titles of,
    150

*Namely,* use of, 92
Names of places, punctuation for,
    147-48
Natural tone, 79-80
    exercises for, 84

*Nearby,* use of, 92
Negative/positive sequence,
    136-37, 138-39
"Negative" words, 83-84
    exercises vs., 85
*Nevertheless,* use of, 92, 145
*Next,* use of, 92, 145
Nicknames, punctuation for
    ("Babe" Ruth), 151
Noise, *see* Interference
Nonproductive written
        communication, 168
Nonrestrictive clauses
    definition of, 145
    punctuation for, 146
*Nor,* use of, 145
*Notwithstanding,* use of, 92

Occupations, technical jargon of,
    47-48
    exercises on, 56-59
*Of,* overuse of, 65-66
*Of course,* punctuation for, 146
Old-fashioned language, 80
Omission of figures or letters,
    punctuation for, 150
*On the other hand,* use of, 92
*On the whole,* use of, 92
Openings, 101, 112-19
    definition of, 113
    exercises in, 125
*Opposite to,* use of, 92
*Or,* use of, 145
Order of ideas, 42-43
Organization
    checklist for, 166
    poor, 22, 100
    *See also* Planning
Organizational sequences, 128-37
    exercises on, 140-41
*Otherwise,* use of, 92, 145
Outlines, 100
    *See also* Planning
Outside, use of, 92
*Over,* use of, 92
Overall approach, 104-109
    direct, 104-109
        closings and, 112, 120-24
        openings and, 116-19

Overall Approach, cont.
exercises in, 110-111, 125-27
indirect, 104, 105, 108-109
closings and, 119-20
openings and, 112-16

Paragraphs, effective, 87-99
developing paragraphs, 94-97
exercises in, 97-99
topic sentences, 87-89
transitional devices, 89-94
Passive vs. active sentence
patterns, 65
exercises in, 69-70
Personal tone, 76-77, 79
exercises for, 84
Phrases
jargon, 54-55
exercises on, 57-58
"movable," 40
in series, punctuation for, 146
wordy, 62
exercises for, 69
Physical appearance of your
document, 165-66
Place, words to indicate, 92
Place-names, punctuation of,
147-48
Planning, 100-42
choice of overall approach,
104-109, 112
closings, 101, 112, 119-24
determination of purpose,
101-104
exercises in, 109-111, 125-27,
139-42
five steps in, 101, 137-38
openings, 101, 112-16
organization of "body," 101, 113,
128-37
percentage of time to be spent
in, 164
*Please be advised*, elimination
of, 63
Plural of figures or letters,
punctuation for, 150
Poems, punctuation for titles of,
150
Positive tone, 83-84
exercises for, 85

Possessive case, punctuation for,
150
Precise words, 35-36
exercises on, 44
"Print-oriented people, 159, 161,
170
Priority sequence, 129, 131-32
reverse, 132-33
Problem/cause/solution sequence,
133-34
Productive Potential Scale, 166-69
Professions, technical jargon of,
47-48
exercises on, 56-59
Pronouns
informal tone through use of,
81
personal tone through use of,
76
possessive, punctuation for,
150
*you* vs. *we*, 26-30
Pronunciation of words, 160-61
Proofreading, 159, 165
Providing a reminder, 114
Providing background
information, 115-16
Punctuation, 22, 143-54
exercises in, 151-54
rules for
apostrophes, 150
colons, 148-49
commas, 145-48
dashes, 149
double quotation marks,
150-51
semicolons, 148
single quotation marks, 151
Purpose of writing, determination
of, 101-104
exercises in, 109-10

Quizzes
on helping readers, 25-26
on spelling, 155-56
on writing attitude, 3-8
*See also* Exercises
Quotations, punctuation for, 147,
150-51

Radio programs, punctuation for titles of, 150
Ranking items by importance, 129, 131-32
  reverse, 132-33
Reading, critical, 9-20
Readers
  appropriate tone for, 22, 74-86
  checklist for, 166
  exercises for, 84-86
  understanding by, 49, 51
  writing for, 21-30
  exercises for, 29-30
Recommendations
  elaborating on, 121
  making, 117-19, 120
  of solutions, sequence for, 133-34
Redundant words, 63
  exercises on, 70
Results, words to indicate, 92
Reverse priority sequence, 132-33
Revising, percentage of time to be spent in, 164-65

Sarcastic tone, 77, 78
Semicolons
  rules for, 148
  use of, 143, 144
Sentences
  combining related elements of, 66-67
  coordination of parts of, 40-42
  dangling parts of, 37-39
  "dummy" subjects for, 63-64
  effective, exercises on, 9-20
  general exercises on, 44-46, 69-70
  hackneyed introductions to, 62-63
  as independent clauses, 145
  logic of, 43-44
  optimum length of, 61, 67
  sentence actors in, 65
  topic, 87-89
  unclear, 22, 31
  which and that clauses in, 39-40
Sequences, organizational, 128-37

Sequences, organizational, cont.
  exercises on, 140-41
Sequential sequence, 130-31
Series, punctuation for, 146, 148-49
Short stories, punctuation for titles of, 150
"Silent eye," 160, 170
Similarly, use of, 92
Simply stated, use of, 92
Single quotation marks, rules for 151
Solutions of problems, sequence for, 133-34
Specific words, 34-35
Specifically, use of, 92
Speeches, punctuation for titles of, 150
Spelling, 22, 155-63
  exercises in, 161-63
  learning rules of, 158-59
  lists of common words misspelled, 155-56, 162
Static, see Interference
Statistical data, 113, 128
Still, use of, 92, 145
"Storytelling," elimination of, 67, 68
Subsequently, use of, 92, 145
Summaries
  punctuation for, 149
  words to indicate, 92
Symbols, plural of, punctuation for, 150

Tactful tone, 82-83
  exercises for, 85
Technical jargon, 47-48
  exercises on, 56-59
That clauses, 39-40
That is, use of, 92
Then, use of, 92, 145
There is, overuse of, 63-64, 79
Therefore
  punctuation for, 146, 148
  use of, 92, 145
Thereupon, use of, 92
Threatening tone, 77
Thus, use of, 92, 145

Time
  to be spent on elements of
      writing, 164
  words to indicate, 92
Titles of speeches, books, etc.,
      punctuation for, 150
*To be,* overuse of, 64-65
*To conclude,* use of, 92
*To illustrate,* use of, 92
*To summarize,* use of, 92
*To the contrary,* use of, 92
*To the right, to the left,* use of, 92
Tone
  checklist for, 166
  inappropriate, 22, 74-86
    exercises for, 84-86
*Too,* use of, 92
Topic sentences, 87-89
Transitional devices, 89-94
  exercises on, 97-99
Transitional words, punctuation
      for, 146-47
TV programs, punctuation for
      titles of, 150


Uncommon words, 53-54
  exercises on, 57
*Under,* use of, 92
Underlining, use of, 150
Understanding, jargon and, 51
*Unfortunately,* punctuation for,
      146
Unintended meanings, 36-37
Unity
  in organizational sequences,
      129
  in paragraphs, 87, 89, 93-94
    exercises in, 97-99
Unnecessary details, 67-69
  exercises on, 70


Vague jargon, 55-56
Vague words, 34-35

*We,* use of, in letters, 26-28, 79,
      81
  exercises in, 29-30
*Which* clauses, 39-40
Word guides, 158, 159
Wordiness, 22, 60-73, 171
  exercises in, 69-73
Words
  ambiguous, 36-37
  coined, punctuation for, 150-51
  common vs. uncommon, 53-54
  correct, 32-34
  emphatic, punctuation for,
      150-51
  exercises on, 44, 56-57
  "inflated," 52-53
  ironic use of, punctuation for,
      150-51
  key, 90-91
  "Latinistic, 50
  "movable," 40
  "negative," 83-84
  possibly misunderstood,
      punctuation for, 147
  precise, 35-36
  pronunciation of, 160-61
  redundant, 63
  in series, punctuation for, 146
  specific vs. general, 34-35
  transitional, 89-94
  *See also* Spelling
Writing attitude, quiz on, 3-8
Writing evaluation, 164-71
  checking overall image, 165-66
  determination of weaknesses,
      169-71
  percentage of time to be spent
      in, 164
  setting up scale, 166-69


*Yet,* use of, 92
*You,* use of, in letters, 26-30, 76,
      79
  exercises in, 29-30